A WORKSHOP ON

The Book of John

CAROLYN NYSTROM

Lamplighter Books Grand Rapids, Michigan
Zondervan Publishing House

Other books by Carolyn Nystrom include:

A Woman's Workshop on Romans
A Workshop on the Christian Faith
A Workshop on David and His Psalms
At the Starting Line: Beginning a New Life
Before I Was Born
Jesus Is No Secret
Lord, I Want to Have a Quiet Time
Mario's Big Question: A Child's Guide Through Adoption
Mike's Lonely Summer
What Is a Christian?
What Is Prayer?
What Is the Bible?
Who Is God?

A Workshop on the Book of John
Copyright © 1989 by Carolyn Nystrom

Lamplighter Books are published by the Zondervan Publishing House
1415 Lake Drive, S.E., Grand Rapids, Michigan 49506

ISBN 0-310-41841-0

Edited by Mary McCormick, John Sloan

Printed in the United States of America

89 90 91 92 93 / LP / 10 9 8 7 6 5 4 3 2 1

CONTENTS

For
Amy, Sue, Dawn, Joan, Lois
Judy N., Judy O., Sandee, and Phil
who helped me try it out

THE BOOK OF JOHN

"The writer of John left the key hanging by the back door," observed a Bible scholar who had studied John's gospel to the end. He pointed, of course, to closing paragraphs of the book where John spoke of his reason for writing.

> Jesus did many other miraculous signs in the presence of his disciples, which are not recorded in this book. But these are written that you may believe that Jesus is the Christ, the Son of God, and that by believing you may have life in his name. (John 20:30–31)

John doesn't record many miracles—only seven, six of them in the first half of the book—but those seven miracles testify to an enormous range of power. What does it take to turn water into wine—and what kind of person would do so? How can a child be healed by a mere spoken word—at a distance of twenty miles? Thirty-eight years is a long time for a person to be an invalid. What would it take to make him well—instantly? Is there a special formula for feeding five thousand people out of one bag lunch, or for walking on water? How can a man who has never seen, not even as a baby, come to physical and spiritual sight—in moments?

These are only a few miracles, interspersed with lucid teaching and verbatim conversation, yet John tells of each event with an eye to the characters. Who were they? How did they get where they were? What were they thinking and feeling? How did they change? But John also points an eye straight at his reader. What does his reader need to know about Jesus in order to believe?

Like the characters in his gospel, it's impossible to study John and remain neutral. Page after page, a reader must ask, "Who is this man called Jesus?" And, "If Jesus is all this book claims, what must I do about His claim on me?"

I'VE JOINED THE GROUP. NOW WHAT?

Here are some guidelines that will help you feel comfortable in a discussion Bible study and, at the same time, grow as a result of your presence there.

1. Take a Bible with you. Any modern translation is fine.

2. Arrive at Bible study on time. It's just a normal courtesy to a group that does its best work when all are together.

3. Come prepared. Read the passage. Ask yourself the questions it raises in your mind. Think about how you might live out its teachings.

4. Call your host(ess) if you are going to be absent. Then the group won't waste time waiting for you.

5. Volunteer to be a host(ess). A quick way to feel that you belong to a group is to have it meet at your house.

6. Don't overtalk or undertalk. Others in the group need your thoughts—but you also need theirs.

7. Keep on track. Stay with a particular passage of

Scripture: what it says, means, and how it touches your life. Refer to previous passages in the book as the need arises.

8. Help pace the study. You should discuss all of the questions in about an hour to an hour and fifteen minutes.

9. Don't criticize another church or religion. This can cause unintentionally hard feelings in a group of mixed backgrounds and beliefs.

10. Get to know people in your group. Some of the best relationships grow out of group Bible studies.

11. Invite others to the group. Any Bible study group grows best as it absorbs new people and new ideas.

12. Get ready to lead. Watching someone else do the job two or three times gives all the experience you need to ask the questions yourself.

ME, A LEADER?

Many Bible study groups have the members share the responsibility of leading the discussion. Here are some guidelines for doing it well.

1. Prepare well ahead of time. Read the Scripture passage. Note possible answers to each question. Then pray by name for each person in your group.

2. Pace the study. Begin on time. Space the questions. End on time.

3. Ask your group to read the passage aloud by paragraphs—not verses. Verse divisions (a relatively recent addition to the text) break the flow of thought and may confuse its meaning.

4. Ask, don't tell. This study guide is designed for a discussion moderated by a leader—not an outline for a lecture.

5. Avoid tangents. Use good sense about whether a

discussion direction takes you from the passage to life, and back again—or whether it is simply irrelevant.

6. Talk about application. Letting God's Word touch your life is worth the extra risk (and time) it takes to discuss these questions together.

7. Try a prayer and share time before or after the study. A few moments of shared needs, thanksgivings, and prayer may mean more in some situations than anything else that you do during your time together.

8. Enjoy leading. It's a rewarding job.

1

THE WORD BECAME FLESH

John 1:1–34

And you, my child, will be called a prophet
*   of the Most High;*
for you will go on before the Lord to prepare
*   the way for him,*
to give his people the knowledge of salvation.
*   (Luke 1:76–77)*

Lofty words for a father to speak to his eight-day-old son. But that's the way John the Baptist started out.

Born six months earlier than Jesus, John and Jesus were relatives—through their mothers—but they had more in common than genes. Both had their coming birth announced by an angel. (An angel spoke to John's father and to Jesus' mother.) Both came by miraculous birth. (John's mother was too old to have children; Jesus' mother was a virgin.) Both had parents who broke into poetry at the thought of their

12

coming. (See Zechariah's Song and Mary's Song, both recorded in Luke 1.) As they grew older, both developed loyal followers, and both had a special mission from God.

Here, however, their similarities began to fade. For Jesus Christ, son of Mary, adopted son of Joseph, was God Himself—in human form. And cousin John? John was a witness. He would prepare the way for Jesus—then quietly drop out of sight.

1. What do you look for in a good witness? _____

_____

Read aloud John 1:1–14.

2. a. What all can you know about the Word from these verses? _____

_____

   b. Why might you want to know a person described in this way? _____

_____

3. What clues in the text help you assign an identity to the Word? _____

_____

4. In what ways is the term "Word" appropriate for this person? _____

_____

5. How do the terms "grace" and "truth" help define Christ's glory? _____

_____

6. People often quote from this opening section of the book of John. What is captivating about this passage? _____

_____

Read aloud John 1:15–34.

7. As you try to imagine the events in these verses, what pictures come to your mind? _____

_____

8. If you had known John, do you think you would have liked him? Why, or why not? _____

_____

Note: The man, John, in this passage is John, the Baptist, a cousin to Jesus through his mother, Mary. He is not John, the writer, who later became a disciple to Jesus.

9. a. What words and phrases here help define John's relationship to Jesus?

_____

   b. What difficulties do you see in John's position? _____

_____

10. Look more carefully at verses 29–34. How did John's introduction of Jesus continue to answer the identity questions of the previous day? _____

_____

11. What did John himself learn by his encounter with Jesus? _____

_____

12. In what ways did John accomplish his self-described mission of verse 23 as a witness to "Make straight the way for the Lord"? _____

_____

13. a. Meditate for a moment on the words of verse 14. How might these words influence your study of the book of John? _____

_____

b. How do they influence your relationship with Jesus?

_____

THIS WEEK

Who has been a witness to you about Jesus Christ? This week make contact with someone who has helped you to know Jesus. Express your appreciation to that person. Discover what new knowledge of Jesus you can experience together.

2

FOLLOW ME

John 1:35–2:25

It must have seemed strange to a few first-century fishermen. One day they were doing routine fish work: mending nets, scraping boats, checking the weather and the market, talking about that crazy but fascinating preacher named John who held crowds at attention out in the desert. The next day the fish nets sat as if to mend themselves and the boats skittered out on the lake in the custody of friends. The fishermen had taken on a new occupation—disciples to Jesus.

Did their mothers worry, their wives complain, their friends plead for a return to normalcy? Or were these new disciples onto something big?—something so big that they simply needed to point those close to them to Jesus, and they, too, enjoyed the wealth of walking in Palestine sand with God in man's sandals.

Today's disciples sometimes endure that same abrupt shift

of scene. One day life is normal, routine, mundane. And the next . . . The next day God Himself invites them to walk with Him, to be His own. Or perhaps the change is slow—a gradual coming to know who Jesus is, not was, but *is*, now and forever, and that His invitation is the same as it was on the shore of a fishing lake two thousand years ago. He says, "Follow Me."

Read aloud John 1:35–51.

1. Find the first four disciples mentioned in John's gospel. How did each come to Jesus? _____

_____

2. Study Christ's response to each of these four men. What might each person have found particularly inviting about Jesus? _____

_____

3. a. How were you first introduced to Jesus? _____

_____

b. Who or what influenced you then to find out more about Jesus? _____

_____

4. Notice four different ways in which witnesses here described Jesus. In what ways are each of these descriptions a "statement of faith"? _____

_____

5. Compare the names for Jesus given in verses 49 and 51. How do Christ's qualities, as described by these names, cause heaven to open? _____

_____

Read aloud John 2:1–11.

6. Would you want to have been a servant at this wedding? Why or why not? _____

_____

7. Locate each character or character group in this event. How does each move the story along? _____

_____

8. Why do you think that Jesus spoke as He did to His mother, but then went on to provide wine? _____

_____

9. How could the disciples know Jesus better because of what they witnessed at this wedding? _____

_____

Read aloud John 2:12–25.

10. If a disciple of Jesus were considering whether to remain with Jesus, what factors would this event cause him to consider? _____

_____

11. In what sense did Christ's words about raising up the temple meet the Jews' demand for a sign of His authority? ___

_____

Read again John 2:11.

12. What do these words convey as the purpose of Christ's miraculous signs? _____

_____

13. a. When you try to imagine Christ's glory, what comes to your mind? _____

_____

b. What aspects of Christ's glory does today's study reveal to you? (Use the whole passage.) _____

_____

14. What have you seen of Christ's work that makes it easier for you to believe in Him? _____

_____

THIS WEEK

The early disciples were so excited about meeting Jesus that they quickly told others and brought them to Jesus, too. This week, try to convey some of your own excitement in learning about Jesus as you invite one new person to your Bible study group.

3

BORN AGAIN

John 3

Born again. It's such a strange term. It conjures all sorts of impossible images. Small wonder a Jewish rabbi felt a little startled when he first heard the term from Jesus.

"Born again" doesn't always set well with twentieth-century audiences, either. The TV evangelist who shouts the words finds ready listeners among those already on his turf, but among the uninitiated . . . ? These he leaves, with a quizzical frown or the flick of a wrist on the dial.

"Born again" is a phrase not frequently used in Scripture. It appears only in John 3. But in that chapter it comes from the lips of Jesus Himself and it comes with a sense of urgency that says, "Listen up!"

1. What feelings does the phrase "born again" bring to your mind? _____

_____

Read aloud John 3:1–15.

2. How did the initial actions and words of Nicodemus suggest that he might be receptive to what Jesus was about to say? _____

_____

3. What reasons did Nicodemus have to be surprised at Christ's response to his visit? _____

_____

4. What words in this passage show that Jesus thought being born again was important? _____

_____

5. How does Christ's illustration of the wind contribute to understanding new birth? _____

_____

6. a. How did Jesus show that He understood how hard it was for Nicodemus to believe? _____

_____

b. What did Jesus add here that might help Nicodemus accept what He said? _____

_____

7. a. See Numbers 21:4–9 for a story Nicodemus would have known from Jewish history. In what ways would Jesus become like that snake? _____

_____

b. Of what value might this reference to a snake become to Nicodemus at a later time? _____

_____

Read aloud John 3:16–21.

8. According to these verses, do people start out rightly or wrongly in their relationship with God? _____

_____

9. What does the illustration of light and darkness suggest as a reason why people might choose not to believe in Jesus?

_____

10. John 3:16 has sometimes been called Christ's message in a nutshell. Examine each phrase of this verse. What does each one contribute to your understanding of Jesus and His purpose? _____

_____

Read aloud John 3:22–36.

11. Why might John the Baptist have felt himself to be in competition with Jesus at this point in his ministry? _____

_____

12. What was John saying about himself when he called himself the "friend of the bridegroom" and the "one who is from earth"? What was he saying about Jesus? _____

_____

13. How do the events in verses 22–36 reinforce Christ's teachings about the way to God? _____

_____

14. Suppose a friend were to say to you, "Jesus can't be the only way to God. He is one of many ways from many world religions." What could you point out from John 3 that shows Jesus and His follower disagreeing with this point of view?

_____

15. According to this chapter, what is at stake pending an individual's response to Jesus? _____

_____

16. In view of this, what action should you take based on the message of John 3? _____

_____

THIS WEEK

Being born again is as simple as A-B-C-D-E.[1] This week, study (really examine with your heart and mind) each of the five steps below. If you have taken each of these steps at some time in your past, thank God again that through Jesus you have been born into His family. If you have missed one or more of these steps, prayerfully consider taking them this week.

A Admit that you are a sinner, and that your sin separates you from God.

B Believe that Jesus died to pay for all of your sin.

C Count the cost of committing to Christ all areas of your life from now on.

D Do it. Tell God in prayer that you repent of all you have done wrong and give yourself wholly to Him.

E Explain to at least one person what you have done, telling him or her that Jesus is now your Lord.

_____

[1] Adapted from *New Life: A Woman's Workshop on the Christian Faith,* by Carolyn Nystrom, Zondervan, 1986. Used by permission.

4

I AM THE CHRIST

John 4:1–42

It was hot—high noon in a small dusty town in the Middle East. Most women used this hot time of the day to rest, play quietly with their children, or perform some small household task in the relative coolness of their homes. Yet one woman trudged alone, a stone water jar on her head, to the community well at the town's edge.

It wasn't the time for drawing water. Most women went to the well together, in the cool of early morning or late evening. Why did this woman go at noon? Had she slept late? Had she not planned her use of water carefully and run out? Was someone ill or inconsiderate about water use in her home, thus forcing an extra trip? Or did she choose, for her own reasons, to come alone—when the well was deserted?

We can't know. But while she was alone at that village well, she met a Man. And there ensued one of the most astounding conversations in all of recorded Scripture.

Read aloud John 4:1–26.

1. How did Jesus happen to be sitting by a well in Sychar?_

_____

2. If you had been this woman, when would you have begun to believe that Jesus cared about you? _____

_____

Why? _____

_____

3. Circle each use of the word "water" in this conversation. How does the meaning Jesus gave to "water" differ from what the woman at first had in mind? _____

_____

4. a. For a history of the tension between Jews and Samaritans regarding where and how to worship, read 1 Kings 12:26–30; 2 Chronicles 11:13–17; and 2 Kings 17:22–33.

Now back to John 4. To what extent did Jesus take sides in this conflict? _____

_____

b. How did Jesus use this conflict to teach the true nature of worship? _____

_____

5. a. What problems would you see in worship that lacks spirit? _____

_____

b. What problems would you see in worship that lacks truth? _____

_____

6. a. Meditate for a moment on the concept of verse 23— that God seeks true worshipers.

What does it mean to you that almighty God invites your worship? _____

_____

b. What would you like to do to improve your worship of God? _____

_____

7. Review all of Christ's conversation with this woman. In what different ways did He help her to believe in Him? _____

_____

8. a. Verses 25 and 26 provide one of the most straightforward statements of Christ's identity in all of Scripture.

What effect would you expect it to have on the woman here? _____

_____

b. What is its effect on you? _____

_____

Read aloud John 4:27–42.

9. In view of what the woman was doing while Jesus spoke with His disciples, what did Jesus mean by "harvest"? _____

_____

10. a. In what ways are the sower and the reaper dependent on each other in this harvest? _____

_____

b. Why might the sower and reaper add to each other's joy? _____

_____

11. a. Why did Jesus stay two days in Sychar? _____

_____

b. With what results? _____

_____

c. How were the people of Sychar different because of Christ's stay with them? _____

_____

12. Compare the woman's ideas about Christ's identity in verses 9, 12, 19, 29, and 42. How is each related to the previous one? _____

_____

13. a. Which of these identities best describes your own view of Jesus? _____

_____

b. If you were to act wholeheartedly on that belief, what would you do? _____

_____

THIS WEEK

One of the reasons that the woman of Samaria learned so much about Jesus was that she took time to talk with Him and to listen to Him. This week, spend some time each day with Jesus. Pray to Him. (He *is* God, you know.) Tell Him your thoughts, feelings, questions, fears. Take courage by knowing that Jesus understands—He was human, too.

Then listen to Jesus. Listen to His words as recorded in the New Testament. (Matthew chapters 5 through 7 is a good place to study some of His teachings, and Luke 8 will reveal some of His actions.) As you learn to know Jesus through prayer and through study, be ready (as was the Samaritan woman) to share this knowledge with your friends.

5

BARRIERS TO BELIEF

John 4:43–5:15

"But I've heard about Jesus all my life. My mother used to make me go to church three times a week. I've had it up to here with religion."

"Hey, I like this Jesus stuff. Just yesterday, I asked Jesus to help me find my car keys. And two minutes later I found them in the silverware drawer. Now who would have guessed . . . "

"Don't preach at me about Jesus. My life is not the best, but I'm the one in charge of it. And right now that's the way I like it."

"I'd like to believe, but I had a terrible childhood: moved every year, my dad left when I was fourteen, my mother slept around. Now I can't trust anybody. Maybe if my past had been different . . . "

"So I said to my kid, 'You come into this house one more with a pack of cigarettes and you'd better start househunting.

I won't have that stuff in my house.' I wish he'd pay attention when I say " 'Jesus loves you. . . .' "

"Sure, I believe in Jesus. He was a great teacher. His words make me feel warm and loving inside. But I don't like all this talk about sin. I haven't killed anybody yet—and as for little sins—they add spice to life. I'm sure Jesus wouldn't mind."

Barriers to belief—all of them. Any faith in Jesus must stand on His true nature, His nature as defined by Scripture. Jesus is not an imaginary god we can create in whatever image suits our needs, for then He would not be God at all.

Yet we build a hundred barriers to belief in Jesus. (So did the people of His day.) But if we are to scramble over those barriers, we must first know who Jesus is.

Read aloud John 4:43–54.

1. What factors contributed to the way the people of Cana felt about Jesus? _____

_____

2. What motives might the people of Cana now have for receiving Jesus? _____

_____

3. What details here suggest the urgency of the royal official's need? _____

_____

4. Why do you think Jesus responded to the father's urgent request with a complaint? (See verse 48.) _____

_____

5. What dilemma did this official face when Jesus told him that his son would live? _____

_____

6. What relevance does distance have to this story? (Use a map.) _____

_____

7. In what different ways did Jesus help the royal official to grow in faith? _____

_____

8. Look again at Christ's complaint of verse 48. To what extent is your own communication with Jesus based on what He can do for you? _____

_____

Read aloud John 5:1–15.

9. What did the invalid man hope to gain by lying near the pool? _____

_____

10. Why do you think Jesus asked the man, "Do you want to get well?" _____

_____

11. In this story what part does time play? _____

_____

12. a. Why did the Jews criticize the healed man? _____

_____

   b. What does this criticism hint of their underlying values? _____

_____

Note on verse 14: Christ's temple encounter with the healed man hints that sin was a cause of the man's long illness. This, of course, is not true in all situations. Jesus, because He is

God, knew the man's heart. Mere humans cause grave damage when they make such accusations.

13. a. Look at both miracles of healing. In what ways did each healed man act out his faith? _____

_____

b. How did the actions themselves increase their faith? _

_____

14. Survey again these two miracles to discover what they reveal of Christ's nature. Give answers that begin, "Jesus is Master over . . . " _____

_____

15. What barriers suggested in these two miracles keep people from knowing Christ's true nature? _____

_____

16. How are you affected by these barriers? _____

_____

THIS WEEK

Do you want to know Jesus better, to receive inner healing from Him that promotes spiritual growth? If so, take stock of the barriers that you have allowed to stand between you and a deep knowledge of Jesus. Choose one, and this week begin to take that barrier apart—brick by brick.

6

FROM DEATH TO LIFE

John 5:16–47

In 588 B.C., the nation of Judah celebrated its 432nd anniversary. It wasn't much of a celebration. Judah's sister nation to the north, Israel, had collapsed 132 years before. Now nations around Judah menaced her borders like vultures.

The biggest threat was Babylon, six hundred miles to the east. Babylon had been a power for two thousand years. Now a nation of vast wealth, culture, and strength, it had conquered much of the known world. Judah was next in line.

Yet God had been warning Judah for centuries. Over and over the people of Judah (Jews) had broken the first command, "You shall have no other gods before me." They had taken up Canaanite gods and Assyrian gods, and even invented their own gods. (A snake on a pole given by Moses to symbolize salvation through the coming Messiah developed a name of its own: Nehushtan. They burned incense to it.) God warned them repeatedly. Prophets railed against the extra gods. Pious kings tore them down. But in months, or years, the gods were back and the people as pagan as ever.

Then came Babylon. In 587 B.C., Babylon conquered Judah. Soldiers took her people first northeast, then southeast over a one-thousand-mile trek to Babylon. There they learned what years of prophets had not been able to teach. In Babylon, a foreign land with foreign gods and their own temple of worship far away, the Jews demonstrated the perversity of human nature and God's own purging through pain, by becoming staunchly monotheistic.

After fifty years in Babylon, a generous Persian king (Persia conquered Babylon) sent the Jews back home. They rebuilt their homes, trimmed their grapevines, reconstructed the temple—and became the strongest defenders of the "one true God" the world had known. Whatever their errors in religious practice, they never again fell into the worship of multiple gods.

Then five hundred years later came Jesus. He was God's long-promised Messiah, some claimed. But who was Jesus, really? If God is only one, how could he have a son? And this Son promised life. Small wonder that Jewish religious leaders were worried.

Read aloud John 5:16–18.

1. What was wrong with Jesus, according to His Jewish critics? _____

_____

Read aloud John 5:19–23.

2. What connections does this paragraph draw between Jesus and God the Father? _____

_____

3. What is the purpose of this close tie between Jesus and His Father? _____

_____

4. How does the Father show love to His Son? _____

_____

5. According to these verses, what all can Christ's hearers anticipate in the future? _____

_____

Read aloud John 5:24–30.

6. Twice Jesus says, "A time is coming." What will happen at that time? _____

_____

7. a. What is at stake in Christ's judgment? _____

_____

    b. How can we escape His judgment? _____

_____

8. In view of all of today's passage thus far, why can Jesus claim at the end, " . . . my judgment is just"? _____

_____

Read aloud John 5:31–40.

9. What different sources of testimony did Jesus call as witness to Himself? _____

_____

10. a. How did the people respond to each witness? _____

_____

b. How might a different response to each witness have led them to Jesus? _____

_____

Note on verse 31: A man's testimony about himself was not, by Jewish law, admissible evidence in court.

11. Who, or what, has been a witness to you about Jesus? _

_____

Read aloud John 5:41–47.

12. a. What reasons would Jewish listeners have to be angry at these words? _____

_____

b. If they saw them as true, what could Jewish listeners have learned from these words? _____

_____

13. a. The principal tenet of Judaism is monotheism (belief in one God). Why would Jesus be a particular threat to this principle? _____

_____

b. How might Christ's teachings here ease that threat? (Use the whole passage.) _____

_____

14. a. Look again at verses 21–30. Circle in your Bible each use of the word "live" or "life." What kind of life was Jesus talking about? _____

_____

b. Where does that life come from? _____

_____

c. How does a person receive that life? _____

_____

15. How does this concept of life differ from the non-Christian view of life? _____

_____

16. What do you find attractive about each of these two opposing views? _____

_____

THIS WEEK

Would you like to know more about the future life after death? Read one of these passages each day this week to enjoy promises of the future for those who belong to Jesus.

Romans 8:12–39

1 John 3:1–3

1 Thessalonians 4:13–5:11

1 Corinthians 15

Revelation 21–22

7

FIVE THOUSAND FOR LUNCH!

John 6:1–24

> *Prove to me that you're no fool—*
> *walk across my swimming pool*
> *If you do that for me*
> *then I'll let you go free*
> *C'mon king of the Jews.*

King Herod dances around Jesus, taunting Him with these lyrics by Tim Rice in his opera *Jesus Christ Superstar.* Jesus declines, with dignity, this opportunity to show off His power. The opera ends, as does Scripture, with crucifixion.

Yet Herod's words nag at modern ears. Did Jesus really walk on water and make bread and fish from crumbs? Or was there some illusion? If He really did perform these acts, what was He saying about Himself? And if I have trouble believing them? Sure, I wouldn't dance and prance and shout like the opera's Herod. But if my doubts are there, so that I grope for other explanations, what am I saying about Jesus—and about myself?

Read aloud John 6:1–15.

1. List each character or group of characters in this account. What does each contribute to the story? _____

_____

2. What part does distance play in this story? (Use a map.)

_____

Note: Sea of Tiberias or Sea of Galilee? They are the same body of water. The city of Tiberias was newly founded in A.D. 22 on the sea's western bank. It was named after the Roman emperor Tiberias. Occasionally the sea also acquired the same name.

3. Why did the people follow Jesus? _____

_____

4. Suppose someone said, "Food for five thousand out of one boy's lunch? I don't think so. I suspect that most people just pulled their own lunches out of their pockets and shared with anyone nearby who didn't happen to have food."

What words from the passage conflict with that point of view? _____

_____

5. If this event really happened in the way it is recorded here, what does it reveal about Christ's power? _____

_____

6. a. Twice John records here that Jesus "gave thanks" before this meal. Why do you think Jesus did this? _____

_____

b. What circumstances make it difficult for you to "give thanks" to God for food? _____

_____

c. When have you found this practice to be of particular value? Why? _____

_____

7. What do Christ's actions of verses 14–15 say about His motives for feeding the people? _____

_____

Read aloud John 6:16–24.

8. Imagine that you are one of the five thousand who participated in the events of this two-day period. Explain your thoughts and feelings at its different stages.

after verse 3 _____

_____

after verse 10 _____

_____

after verse 13 _____

_____

after verse 15 _____

_____

after verse 22 _____

_____

after verse 24 _____

_____

9. Suppose someone said, "Walk on water? I don't believe it! Perhaps Jesus was standing on a sandbar, or maybe He followed the boat along the shoreline." What information in the text casts doubt on this point of view? _____

_____

10. If you had been a disciple, why might you be afraid to take Jesus into the boat? _____

_____

11. Why do you think the crowd responded as it did? _____

_____

12. Review briefly John 5:19–23. What links can you find between the two miracles of John 6 and the claims of Jesus in John 5? _____

_____

13. If you had been a disciple who experienced these two days with Jesus, what would you have learned about Him? __

_____

14. What questions would you still want to ask? _____

_____

THIS WEEK

Would you like to follow Jesus' pattern of giving thanks? If so, post a thank-you reminder in places that often catch your eye. Bring frequently to your mind the thought that all that you have and all that you are comes from God. Then thank Him: for your car, for a white cloud overhead, for rain on your window, for flowers by a roadside—whatever strikes you as a gift from Him. Make mealtime a special time of worshipful thanks as you acknowledge that your food, whether crackers and cheese or filet mignon, is God's expression of His care for you.

8

BREAD OF LIFE

John 6:25–71

"Eat my flesh and drink my blood." What an offensive invitation to naive followers of Jesus who were only looking for a free meal or two in the desert! Yet Jesus used the hunger in their stomachs to turn their minds toward an even greater need: the hunger in their souls.

Two millennia later, my own church renews history by taking part in the Scottish form of communion. On those occasions, a table surrounded by chairs sits at the front of our sanctuary. Two elders stand at the table. While the congregation sings hymns about Christ's gift to us, we move in small groups to the front—taking time to wait for each other, helping an elderly person up the steps—and sit down at the table to be served Christ's meal.

An elder hands the tray of wafers saying to each of us, eye to eye (I to I), "This is the body of Christ, which was broken for you." And then the wine, "This cup is the new covenant of Christ's blood."

We eat and drink, remembering again Christ's love in this uniquely personal act, and then leave our places at table to make room for others.

But back then, two thousand years ago, in the Galilean sea village of Capernaum, followers of Jesus heard only the first whisper of what this ceremony would come to mean. It began with Christ's words, "I am the bread of life."

Read aloud John 6:25–71.

1. Divide Christ's teachings here into three sections. To whom was He speaking in each? _____

_____

Look more carefully at verses 25–40.

2. Study the series of questions and answers between Jesus and the people. What differences do you see between what the people wanted from Jesus and what He wanted to give? __

_____

3. a. How was Jesus similar to Moses? _____

_____

b. If the people expected Jesus to be another Moses, why might they have been disappointed? _____

_____

4. Circle each use of the word "believe" in these verses. Of what importance is this belief? _____

_____

5. How did Jesus explain the fact that not all of His hearers would believe? _____

_____

6. a. Think for a moment about bread—particularly the bread Jesus had given these people on the other side of the lake. How is Jesus like that bread? _____

_____

b. What did Jesus mean when He said, "I am the bread of life"? _____

_____

7. a. Meditate on the words of verse 35. What do you think Jesus meant the words "hunger" and "thirst" to symbolize?

_____

b. If you have believed in Jesus and thereby received this bread, in what ways have you seen it satisfy hunger and thirst? _____

_____

Study again John 6:41–59.

8. What doubts about Jesus did the Jews express? (Look for their questions and the implications behind those questions.)

_____

9. Examine verses 43–51 with these questions.

a. How did Jesus explain lack of faith among these Jews?

_____

_____

b. What connections did Jesus draw between Himself and God the Father? _____

_____

c. What differences did Jesus explain between the manna in the desert and the bread He offered? _____

_____

10. Circle all the uses of the words "life" or "living" in verses 47–59. How are these many uses of life and living related to each other? _____

_____

11. When you consider the purpose for which Jesus died, what do you think He meant by "eat my flesh and drink my blood"? _____

_____

12. Study verse 51, the heart of Christ's teaching to these Jews. If they had accepted these words, what all could they know of Jesus? _____

_____

Read again verses 60–71.

13. a. Why do you think Christ's disciples said, "This is a hard teaching"? _____

_____

b. What do you find difficult about these teachings? ____

_____

14. a. Why did some of the disciples reject what Jesus offered? _____

_____

b. Why did some disciples decide to stay with Jesus? ____

_____

15. Look again at Peter's claim of faith in verses 68–69. If you have chosen to follow Jesus, what prompted you to make that decision? _____

_____

THIS WEEK

Write a letter to Jesus this week.

If you have already given yourself to Him, let your letter become an act of praise. (Peter's words of John 6:68–69 could form an outline.) Let your letter also express your thanks for specific ways that Jesus has met your "hunger" and "thirst." Let the final section express honestly your commitment to Jesus as you give again to Him not only what you were in the past, but also what you have become.

If you have not yet accepted Jesus as your own bread of life and thereby given yourself wholly to Him, you also should write a letter to Jesus. Tell Him of your questions and doubts and hesitations. Ask Him, if you are willing, to overcome these and draw you to Himself.

When you have finished writing, read your letter to Jesus as a prayer.

9

LIVING WATER

John 7

Last summer I hiked with two of our children in the Copper Falls area of northern Wisconsin. We had driven two hours from our rented cottage through peaked pines reaching through clear blue sky—bluer than any sky in our native Illinois. We deliberately took forest roads, so rarely saw buildings or even other cars in that two hours. It was a day for God's unembellished nature.

"The falls are beautiful," we'd been told, "well worth the drive. You can't imagine the power of all that water tumbling down cliffs and over rocks."

Once there, we parked the car and followed the hiking-trail signs. By the time we'd hiked even twenty minutes, I noticed that teenage bodies handle hiking uphill a lot better than mid-forty bodies. Surely hiking had been a lot easier a couple of years back. And six years ago, *I'd* been prodding *them* to keep up!

"I wish I'd been more patient back then," pricked at my mind as the kids slowed their pace and admired wildflowers so I could catch up under averted eyes.

But soon we heard the roar of the water up ahead. At first it was so low and so steady, we weren't sure it was water. A nearby factory? An airplane? But even then the sound projected massive power. As we hiked closer, we could hear the enormous range of tones—high and tinkly, low rushing, slamming against boulders. My hot feet begged for a fresh clear spatter from this gigantic sound. I hoped the trail would take us right to the edge.

Then, through a break in the trees, we sighted the boiling river. Water churned and raged and exploded its way over mountainous boulders on its path downstream. Yet we stopped at the cliff top unmotivated to scramble the few steps down to its brink. For all of its power, the river was dead: brown-stained murk from copper strip mines.

We watched it for a while from our distant point of view, pondering our disappointment. Then we hiked back down the trail.

A trickle of warm water from a nearby drinking fountain quenched our thirst. (At least it was clean.) Then we drove home.

Water attracts us. From it, we expect rest and refreshment and sustenance and power. So when Jesus offered Himself as a gift to believers, He used the metaphor of water—living water.

Read again John 6:66–69.

1. What changes would you expect to see in the people who positioned themselves on each of these two sides? _____

Read aloud John 7:1–13.

2. What differences do you see between the perspectives of Jesus and His brothers when they talked about whether to go to Jerusalem? _____

_____

3. What different effects did Christ's visit to Jerusalem have on the people there? _____

_____

4. Take one of these responses and defend it as might a twentieth-century person who knew of Jesus. _____

_____

Read aloud John 7:14–44.

5. a. Which of Christ's actions in Jerusalem do you find surprising for a person who wanted to avoid publicity? _____

_____

b. Why do you think Jesus prompted this public confrontation? _____

_____

c. What evidence do you see that the conflict between Jesus and unbelievers had grown beyond mere disagreement? _____

_____

6. a. Look more carefully at verses 14–24. What conflict do you see between Christ's source of teaching and the crowd's explanation of His source? _____

_____

b. If anyone chose to do God's will, as Jesus invited in verse 17, what all would that person have discovered? (Use this whole section.) _____

_____

c. What contrast did Jesus draw between His brothers' motives for getting Him to Jerusalem and His own motives for coming? _____

_____

7. a. Look more carefully at verses 25–43. In what different ways did the people question Christ's origins? _____

_____

b. Why was Christ's origin an important question? _____

_____

8. a. Find as many clues as you can that Jesus would not be with these people long. What did He want them to know about His future? _____

_____

b. How might this information about the future affect their current response to Him? _____

_____

Read aloud John 7:32 and 45–52.

9. a. Why wasn't Jesus arrested? _____

_____

b. What did even this mild defense of Jesus cost the temple guards and Nicodemus? _____

_____

Study again John 7:37–39.

   10. a. What invitation did Jesus extend? _____

_____

   b. What qualities would you expect to see in a person who responded to this invitation? _____

_____

   11. Tell of a time when you have been refreshed by this living water—either in yourself or in someone else. _____

_____

THIS WEEK

   Do streams of living water flow from you? This week, find a dry place that your life touches. Is a neighbor lonely because she is tied down with young children—or because she is old? Does your local school board need an enthusiastic supporter of special programs for students who are physically or mentally slow? Does your town's governing body need an advocate for people who lack local prestige? Does your church need fresh ideas for worship or a willing set of hands for some lackluster program?

   Choose one of these (or some other) desert areas. Then draw on the living water that Jesus is giving you as you bring new life to a place of thirst.

10

LIGHT OF THE WORLD

John 8:1–30

> *If I say, "Surely the darkness will hide me and the*
> *light become night around me,"*
> *even the darkness will not be dark to you; the*
> *night will shine like the day, for darkness is as*
> *light to you.*

King David, about one thousand years before Christ, wrote this of his God. In Psalm 139, he wrote with great poetic beauty first of God's power of all-knowledge. Next he wrote of God's constant presence. He wrote of trying to run from God, to escape that all-encompassing presence. Surely, in such an attempt, darkness would be his friend and cover him from God's persistent eye. But David discovered, perhaps to his own relief, that "darkness is as light to you."

Later, in this same poem of praise, David invited his all-seeing God to turn the floodlight on him, even his inner self and "Search me . . . ; test me. . . ."

One thousand years later, Jesus talked with skeptical Jews. They couldn't seem to understand who He was. So, with a backward look at David's description of God in Jewish poetry, Jesus declared to these literate Jewish people, "I am the light of the world."

Read aloud John 7:53–8:11.

1. If you were this woman, what all would you feel? _____

_____

2. Read Leviticus 20:10 to discover the law that these religious leaders had in mind. Why do you think they brought the woman—but not the man? _____

_____

3. What do you think the religious leaders hoped Jesus would do? _____

_____

4. Why do you think the religious leaders drifted away as they did? (See Deuteronomy 17:2–7 for legal instructions on execution by stoning.) _____

_____

5. a. What contrasts do you see between the way the religious leaders treated this woman and the way Jesus did?

_____

   b. How can you explain these differences? _____

_____

6. What lasting effects do you think this event had on the woman? _____

_____

Read aloud John 8:12–30.

   7. a. Why did the Pharisees doubt Christ's testimony? _____

---

   b. How did Jesus explain their doubt? (See especially verses 13–20.) _____

---

   8. Look more carefully at Christ's statement of verse 21. If one of these Jews had been close to belief in Jesus, what would he have found here to be concerned about? _____

---

   9. Do you think Christ's words of verses 23–24 were an angry retort or a compassionate warning? Why? _____

---

   10. Look again at the people's question in verse 25. In what ways would Christ's answer help them to identify Him? _

---

   11. Why do you think many believed in Jesus at this point?

---

   12. What reasons do you have to believe in Jesus? _____

---

   13. Look again at Christ's statement of verse 12 about His identity. In what ways do you think of Jesus as "the light of the world"? _____

---

   14. In what ways does Jesus bring light to your life? _____

THIS WEEK

Draw a chart of your life to this point using a line to indicate the highs and lows. (A wedding or birth of a child might be high points. Divorce or job loss or death of someone close might be lows.)

Then meditate on how Jesus has been light to you—even in those dark times. List some specific events that remind you of His continued presence, both in the light and in the dark. (Was a time of light more intense because Jesus illuminated its meaning? How? Was a time of darkness less desperate because Jesus blunted its pain? How?)

When you have finished this remembering on paper, offer a prayer of praise to Jesus not only because He is the light of the world, but also because He is light to you.

11

WHO DO YOU THINK YOU ARE?

John 8:31–59

When our oldest daughter was approaching her wedding date, I devised a couple of gifts I thought especially appropriate for this new stage in her life. I dug out a large picture of my grandmother (her great-grandmother) at age five and had it framed. Then I wrote on the back all I knew of her genealogical past—along with brief anecdotes to accompany the names and dates: a reverend here, a pioneer there, a Civil War soldier somewhere else. Then I added four sections to my journal for her: my own rememberings of each of her four great-grandparents on my side of the family.

There is a sense in which we are part of these parents from our distant past. It seemed right that she should have some tangible evidence of these qualities that she brought to her marriage.

Jesus, too, had to deal with the issue of biological and spiritual roots. Was He the Son of God? Or was He, as His accusers implied, the son of an unknown father or even of the devil? Eventually they asked point blank, "Who do you think you are?"

Read aloud John 8:31–47.

1. According to Jesus, what must be the first step for a person who has begun to believe in Him? _____

_____

2. a. Why was this next step difficult for Christ's Jewish listeners? _____

_____

   b. Why is it difficult for you? _____

_____

3. How did Christ's teaching about freedom and slavery differ from what these Jews had in mind? _____

_____

4. When have you seen sin cause slavery to itself? _____

_____

5. Who did these Jews claim as their father? _____

_____

6. a. What reasons did Jesus give to show that they could not possibly claim Abraham in their spiritual lineage? _____

_____

   b. What qualities linked them to Satan rather than to God? _____

_____

7. What does it mean to belong to God? _____

_____

8. How can a person who partly believes Jesus still belong to the devil? _____

_____

Read aloud John 8:48–59.

9. a. Why did these Jews object to Christ's words, " . . . if a man keeps my word, he will never see death"? _____

_____

b. What do you think Jesus meant by that statement? _____

_____

10. Why did these Jews question Christ's age? _____

_____

11. a. Consider Christ's statement, "Your father Abraham rejoiced at the thought of seeing my day; he saw it and was glad." What does this statement reveal about Abraham? _____

_____

b. What does it reveal about Jesus? _____

_____

12. Read Exodus 3:13–14 to discover the history behind Christ's words, "Before Abraham was born, I am." In view of this, why did the Jews pick up stones to kill Jesus? _____

_____

13. Look again at the question to Jesus of verse 53, "Who do you think you are?" How would you answer that question about Jesus? (Use with a quotation from John's gospel, if you can, to support your answer.) _____

_____

14. If Jesus was all that John said that He was, what difference does it make to you? _____

_____

THIS WEEK

Jesus said in John's gospel, "I am the Light of the World," "I am the Bread of Life," "I am." Write as many other names for Jesus as you can. Meditate on the meaning of each name. Then praise Jesus by creating a song or art poster that incorporates these names. Use your creation as an aid to worship.

12

I WAS BLIND BUT NOW I SEE!

John 9

> *Amazing grace! how sweet the sound,*
> *That saved a wretch like me!*
> *I once was lost, but now am found,*
> *Was blind but now I see.*　　　*John Newton, 1779*

Personal testimony, eyewitness. It's always been a convincing way to convey a message. Chapter 9 of John's gospel takes a break from the intellectual arguments of previous chapters and says, "Wait a minute; this is what happened." Then John records gesture-by-gesture the actions, and word-by-quoted-word the conversation. And, paradoxically, he lets the reader see all the events through the eyes of a blind man.

1. What is difficult about being close to a person who is blind? _____

_____

Read aloud John 9.

2. How might Christ's method of healing this man be especially helpful to a person in his condition? _____

_____

3. What particular difficulties did this healing present? ____

_____

4. Notice the different ways people in this story viewed the blind beggar.

a. What did the disciples see in the blind man? _____

_____

b. What did his neighbors see? _____

_____

c. What did his own parents see? _____

_____

d. What did the Pharisees see in him? _____

_____

e. How did Jesus see him? _____

_____

5. "Rabbi, who sinned, this man or his parents, that he was born blind?" When have you heard or thought a similar question? _____

_____

6. What added perspective does this story bring to suffering? _____

_____

7. Trace the stages of belief in the blind man by examining each of his statements about Jesus. _____

_____

8. When, in your past, have you experienced one or more of these stages of belief in Jesus? _____

_____

9. Which of these stages best expresses your current view of Jesus? _____

_____

10. Look again at verses 39–41. In what sense did the seeing Pharisees become blind because of this event? _____

_____

11. a. What did Christ's claim, "I am the light of the world" (verse 5), mean to the blind man at the beginning of the story? _____

_____

b. What did the same claim mean to him at the end? ____

_____

12. In what ways was the healed blind man an effective witness? _____

_____

13. If you were to follow this man's example regarding your own experience with Jesus, what would you say and do? _____

_____

THIS WEEK

Today's followers of Jesus can be agents of His healing. This week, think of one person who needs healing from physical pain, emotional loss, a broken relationship, or grief. Then think of practical ways you can help this person, trying to keep in mind his or her perspective—not merely your own. (Jesus used sound and touch for a man who couldn't see.) Spend time and energy this week with this person knowing that Jesus may use you, along with many others, to bring about new health.

13

THE GOOD SHEPHERD

John 10

"Sheep are stupid," said my friend with farm experience. "If one of them takes into its head to fall off a cliff, the others will trail right along behind."

She may have exaggerated a bit in the slander of one of her less favorite farm creatures, but though many people give sheep prizes for cuddly vulnerability, few give them high marks for I.Q.

Why, then, would Jesus compose an allegory in which He poses Himself as shepherd and His people as (you guessed it) sheep? Surely He did not mean to imply that people who follow Him are stupid. Perhaps, instead, He meant us to look at the relationship between the shepherd and his sheep, and in doing so to see what the all-powerful God offers to His people.

Read aloud John 10:1–21.

1. What does a good shepherd do? (Find all that you can.)_

_____

2. How is Jesus like this good shepherd? _____

_____

3. If you were a sheep, why would you want this kind of shepherd? _____

_____

4. How is Jesus also like a gate? _____

_____

5. a. What intruders also have contact with the sheep? _____

_____

b. How is each of these characters different from the shepherd? _____

_____

6. What warnings do you think Jesus was giving to His followers when He spoke of these intruders? _____

_____

7. Study more carefully verses 14–18. What do these verses reveal about the manner and purpose of Christ's death? _____

_____

8. Why were the Jews divided over Christ's words? _____

_____

9. In view of all of this section of John 10, what words would you use to describe the relationship between the

shepherd and his sheep? _____

_____

10. a. Which of these words also describes your relationship to Jesus? _____

_____

b. Tell about one of your own experiences that reflects this description of your relationship with Jesus. _____

_____

Read aloud John 10:22–42.

11. How did Jesus answer their request? _____

_____

12. Why did some not believe Jesus? _____

_____

13. What encouragement to belief did Jesus offer? _____

_____

14. Survey several of Christ's claims about His identity: John 10:30; John 10:36; John 4:25–26; John 9:35–37. Give a summary statement that answers the question, Who did Jesus claim to be? _____

_____

15. Look more carefully at verses 27–30. What words and phrases define the length of Christ's relationship with His people? _____

_____

16. Reread verses 27–30 thoughtfully. How do they make you feel? Why? _____

_____

THIS WEEK

David, the Old Testament psalmist, prepared his readers to receive Jesus as their shepherd. Read psalm 23 every day this week. Each day choose a different line of the psalm as a focus of meditation to keep in front of your mind throughout your day. On the last day, use your favorite musical arrangement of this psalm to sing a prayer of praise to God.

14

LAZARUS, COME FORTH!

John 11

My friend Bob stood beside his wife in front of her mother's casket. He had loved this woman—almost as much as his own mother. With the soft chords of "Amazing Grace" still echoing in his mind, he heard the visiting pastor quote these words of Jesus:

> I am the resurrection and the life. He who believes in me will live, even though he dies; and whoever lives and believes in me will never die. Do you believe this?

Bob believed those words. He had believed them as a child. But that day of his wife's mother's funeral, Christ's words carried new import: believe . . . resurrection . . . life . . . never die. Those were high stakes. If they really reflected the good news of Jesus, Bob wanted to be part of it—forever. From that moment in front of a casket, Bob determined to become a minister of the gospel. I'm glad. He has been my pastor these past twelve years.

1. What kinds of things make you want to cry? _____

_____

Read aloud John 11:1–16.

2. a. How would you describe the relationship between Jesus and the family of Lazarus? _____

_____

   b. Between Jesus and His disciples? _____

_____

3. How did Jesus view the events in Bethany differently from the other people in this story? _____

_____

Note: What did Jesus mean in verse 9 by His question, "Are there not twelve hours of daylight?"

"The *twelve hours in the day* signify the time allotted by the Father for the earthly ministry of Jesus. During those 'hours' neither He nor His disciples can come to any harm. When darkness falls, another 'hour' will have come, the hour for the passion." (Tasker, page 142).

4. Why do you think Jesus stayed where He was for two more days? _____

_____

Read aloud John 11:17–37.

5. Mary, Martha, and several Jews all expressed regret that Jesus had not come sooner. What beliefs and what questions does this regret display? _____

_____

6. What expressions of Christ's love do you see throughout this passage? _____

_____

7. Think of one situation that makes you sad. What practical difference would it make if you could feel that Jesus cares about that hurt—and weeps with you? _____

_____

8. a. Study Christ's conversation with Martha in verses 21–27. Why do you think these words are often read at Christian funerals? _____

_____

b. How might Christ's words here speak to your own fears of death? _____

_____

Read aloud John 11:38–44.

9. a. If you had been in the crowd outside the tomb of Lazarus, what thoughts and feelings would you have experienced? _____

_____

b. What questions would remain in your mind? _____

_____

10. How would you define the purpose of these events in Bethany? (Compare information from verses 4, 14, 27 and 41, 42.) _____

_____

Read aloud John 11:45–57.

11. What dilemma did the Jewish leaders face? _____

_____

12. a. What did Caiaphas mean by his statement? _____

_____

b. Why do you think John recorded it here? _____

_____

13. Review John 1:12. Compare it with John 11:51–52. How might the relationship described here affect the way you express grief over your own losses? _____

_____

THIS WEEK

Mary and Martha talked with Jesus about their brother's death. He shared the loss and cried with them. This week talk to Jesus about a loss that makes you sad. Remind yourself that Jesus loves you and shares that loss with you. Find encouragement in His comfort to Martha in John 11:25–26.

15

HOSANNA!

John 12:1–19

Incense, long white robes trimmed in gold, highbacked bishop's chair, psalms chanted by a cantor, lofty ceiling arched with murals. Stand, sit, kneel, respond. A friend was being ordained as a priest in the Episcopal Church. He had chosen the newly renovated Cathedral of St. James of Chicago as the site for his two-hour ceremony of ordination. Since my own church is somewhat less liturgical, I felt challenged just getting my body in the right positions at the right times. Even so, I could hardly miss the eloquent words of praise full of deep meaning throughout the service. This was worship—not of men and robes and art and music—but of Jesus Christ.

By contrast, I remember a service held in our own backyard when I was a little girl. My mom and dad roused my two sisters and me on Easter Sunday while the sky was still predawn gray. I walked out in dew-soaked bare feet and shivered in the the morning chill just as the women of two thousand years ago must have done. We watched the sun peek over our garden dahlias as my father read to our family, some of us still in night clothes, "Early on the first day of the week, while it was still dark, Mary of Magdala went to the tomb and saw that the stone had been removed." And later the triumphant cry, "The Lord is risen. He is risen indeed." This, too, was worship of our risen Lord.

Worship comes in a variety of colors—these and many others.

1. When you think of worship, what pictures come to your mind? _____

_____

Read aloud John 12:1–11.

2. Name each character in this account. What do you see as the major concern of each? _____

_____

3. Assume for a moment that you have experienced the events of the previous chapter. How would you feel about sitting around the table with these people? _____

_____

4. In what ways do you see death as a theme at this table? _

_____

5. Study more carefully both Mary and Judas. What opposite character traits do you see in them? _____

_____

6. If you had been in that room, how would you feel toward Mary? Toward Judas? _____

_____

7. Jesus quoted from Deuteronomy 15:11 when He answered Judas's complaint. Look up the entire quotation. Do you think Jesus was saying that it is all right to neglect the poor because there is no end to poverty? Explain. _____

_____

8. When have you seen a person give something of great value to Jesus? (Consider time, money, relationships, opportunity.) _____

_____

9. What are some ways you would like to show love to Jesus? _____

_____

Read aloud John 12:12–19.

10. In what different ways do you see worship expressed throughout John 12? _____

_____

11. How was the crowd both an asset and a liability to Jesus? _____

_____

12. Verse 13 is a small part of a song that Jewish pilgrims had sung for hundreds of years on their way to Jerusalem to celebrate Passover. Read aloud Psalm 118:19–27. In what ways does Jesus match the description in this psalm? _____

_____

13. Study Zechariah 9:9. How does John's reference to this prophecy help explain what the disciples later understood? __

_____

14. How was treating Jesus as a king both confusing and enlightening? _____

_____

15. How can we express that Jesus is "King" in our own various acts of worship? (Consider your thoughts and actions in church as well as the various ways you can worship Jesus throughout the week.) _____

_____

THIS WEEK

This week, consider different ways you can express a love for Jesus. Be conscious of Jesus, your King, as you teach your children, as you speak with your boss, as you serve a customer, as you respond to a political issue, as you turn your television on (or off). Bring this backlog of information with you as you prepare for weekly structured worship with others from your church.

16

FATHER, GLORIFY YOUR NAME

John 12:20–50

"I'm not running," said Eric Liddell. The year was 1924. The twenty-two-year-old Scottish runner had been preparing to run the Olympic one-hundred-meter dash for over three years. Preliminary races showed him the best available for that distance—and that distance the best for his strengths.

Then the race schedule was posted. The qualifying heats for one hundred meters were scheduled for Sunday. And Sunday was a day Liddell believed God had reserved for worship and rest. He would not race. Newspapers hooted. Teammates pleaded. But Eric Liddell went to church.

Chariots of Fire, the movie about this event, tells the result. Eric Liddell passed up the one-hundred-meter race, entered the four-hundred-meter instead and, with a roaring crowd to cheer him on, broke all existing records. It was a glorious moment in history.

But the book *Eric Liddell* by D. P. Thompson, a source for

Chariots of Fire, tucks this momentous event into a few brief paragraphs midchapter only one-quarter into the book. Bad writing? Maybe. But Thompson's book emphasizes a different kind of glory: Eric's twenty years of work in China as a missionary of the Christian faith and—in a Japanese internment camp—his death at age forty-three of a brain tumor.

No roaring crowds here. Only sad notes of appreciation to his wife and three small daughters waiting out the war in Canada—and a prisoner's grave in China. Glory? If so, it's viewed through the other end of our human telescope.

1. What images come to your mind when you think of "glory"? _____

_____

The apostle John said that Christ's disciples did not fully understand the events of Palm Sunday until after Jesus had been "glorified" (verse 16). Here Jesus begins to tell His disciples about His immediate future.

Read aloud John 12:20–36.

2. What all did Jesus mean when He said that He was about to be "glorified"? _____

_____

3. In what ways can you see Christ's coming death as both a disgrace and a glory? _____

_____

4. What did Jesus mean when He compared His coming death to a seed? _____

_____

5. What choices do the terms "light" and "darkness" convey to the people who follow Jesus? _____

_____

6. If you had been one of Christ's disciples and had to decide at this point whether to continue to follow Jesus, what particulars would you consider? _____

_____

7. What difficult choices have you had to make regarding your own relationship to Jesus? _____

_____

8. What temptations do you think confronted Jesus at this point in His ministry? _____

_____

Read aloud John 12:37–50.

9. What connections can you see here between Jesus and God the Father? _____

_____

10. According to John's quotations from Isaiah, what are some dangers of unbelief in Jesus? _____

_____

11. What words of caution did Jesus have for "closet Christians"? _____

_____

12. Is believing in Jesus easy or hard for you? Explain. _____

_____

13. Study again verses 42–43. What actions in today's world would gain praise from people—but not from God?

_____

14. Jesus, even when viewing His own execution, prayed in verse 28, "Father, glorify your name." When you encounter points of tension between human glory and God's glory, how can you express your own belief in Jesus? _____

_____

_____

THIS WEEK

The apostle Paul wrote to the church in Corinth, "So whether you eat or drink or whatever you do, do it all for the glory of God" (1 Corinthians 10:31).

This week, be conscious of what you do and say that reflects God's glory. Notice also His glory in other aspects of His creation—people as well as nonhuman creations. (King David found God's glory in a thunderstorm. See Psalm 29.) At the end of the week, write a prayer that speaks to God about some of your experiences.

17

LOVE ONE ANOTHER

John 13

My father's tiny rural church, when he was a boy, practiced foot washing. It was a simple ceremony enacted by simple people with work-weary feet. Men and women (in separated groups) gathered in a circle of chairs. Then calloused knees bent to rough floor planks as fingers removed dusty shoes, poured cool water, washed with soft cloths, dried with coarse sunbleached towels. Old, young, landlord, tenant: each one had a turn. Wash and be washed.

Sure, a few people carefully washed their own feet at home just before they left—a small pride—but, during the ceremony itself, it was hard to feel anything but humble, no matter which side of the washbasin you were on.

Most Christians prefer to remember Christ's example of washing feet in more symbolic ways. But the import of His actions remains. By means not always self-exalting, Jesus tells us to love one another.

1. People who follow Jesus are supposed to love each other.

Why is this hard? _____

_____

Why is it good? _____

_____

Read aloud John 13.

2. John says in verse 1 that Jesus now showed His disciples the full extent of His love. In what different ways do you see Christ showing love in this chapter? _____

_____

Note: One of the less obvious demonstrations of Christ's love is the timing of His teachings. This chapter begins a four-chapter section of "final teachings." Jesus used these as a loving preparation to help His dearest friends through their coming trauma.

Look more carefully at verses 1–17.

3. If you were sitting in that circle of disciples waiting for Jesus to wash your feet, what would you be thinking? _____

_____

What do you think Peter felt? _____

_____

What do you think Judas felt? _____

_____

4. Study verse 3 to see what Jesus knew about Himself. In view of this, why do you think Jesus washed His disciples' feet? _____

_____

5. What is hard about washing someone else's feet—literally? Symbolically? _____

_____

6. Jesus said in verse 14 that we should wash one another's feet. What are some ways you could "wash feet" in your family? _____

_____

In your church? _____

_____

Look more carefully at verses 18–31.

7. What different emotions do you sense among the people mentioned in this scene? _____

_____

8. Why do you think Jesus dipped bread with Judas? _____

_____

9. The symbol of communion (shared bread) also became the symbol of betrayal. How might this influence your own preparation for communion? _____

_____

Focus on verses 31–38.

10. In view of your previous study, what all do you think Jesus meant here when He used the word "glory" in verses 31–32? _____

_____

11. What did Peter not fully understand about Jesus? _____

_____

About himself? _____

_____

12. Study the "new commandment" of verses 34–35. Think again of the ways Jesus showed love to His disciples. How might His disciples show love to each other in similar ways? _____

_____

13. How might people who observe this love between Christ's disciples benefit from it? _____

_____

14. a. Who needs to benefit from your love? _____

_____

b. How can you live out Christ's love in that setting? ____

_____

THIS WEEK

Bring to mind a Christian who has symbolically washed your feet. Send a note to that person to express your appreciation. Or, pass Christ's love along and wash someone else's feet.

18

I WILL NOT LEAVE YOU ORPHANS

John 14

When I was in college, I spent my school breaks working in an orphanage. It was a home for families of servicemen, before the days of foster homes, so almost any child who experienced family losses (divorce, death of a parent, a parent in jail, even an economic slump) might wind up as an "orphan."

Yet Sundays found the rolling grassy lawns crowded with visitors: aunts, uncles—and parents. So, many of these children saw their stay at the orphanage as temporary. They said things like, "My mom is going to have a new apartment by Christmas. I'll go home then." And, "When I'm ten and don't need a baby sitter anymore, then I'm going to live with my dad." And, "When my cousin Janice gets married, I can have her room and live with my aunt and uncle." For them, the orphan stage was temporary.

But there were a few sad children who made no such

plans. No visitors came for them on Sundays. No special boxes arrived for them just days before Christmas. In the long row of wooden toy chests, theirs were empty—except perhaps for a Sunday school paper cutout. They were the true orphans. Their parents were dead.

Sure, we houseparents made special efforts for these kids. We spent time with them on Sundays, bought them special treats, took them home with us for visits. But we could not make up for what they had lost.

When Jesus was about to die, He realized the deep loss His followers would suffer, and He began to prepare them to endure that—to endure the loss and move on to continued fruitful work. And with this preparation was the promise, "I will not leave you as orphans."

Assume for a moment that you are one of Christ's disciples. You have just learned that, through no fault of His own, Jesus will soon be executed. Furthermore, among your own inner circle, one person will betray Him and another will deny Him. Then Jesus speaks.

Read aloud John 14.

1. If you had been one of Christ's disciples, what comfort would you find here? _____

_____

2. What worries do you sense behind Thomas's question? (See verses 1–5.) _____

_____

3. Study Christ's statement of verse 6. If He had instead said, "I *know* or I *teach* the way, the truth, and the life," how would its meaning be different? _____

_____

4. How do Christ's words of verse 6 affect your view of people who follow the non-Christian religions of the world? _

_____

5. What influence do you want the concepts of verse 6 to have on your own relationship with Jesus? _____

_____

6. Are you satisfied by the way Jesus answered Philip's question? Explain. _____

_____

7. How might Christ's words of verses 12–14 grant the disciples purpose for living—even after Jesus was gone?

Note on verse 14: Can we ask God for anything and get it—as long as we mouth the words, "In Jesus' name," at the end? To pray in Christ's name implies a oneness with Him in our desires as well as our words. God will grant what we ask in His name—to the extent that these requests match Christ's purpose and design. Yet, even our most well intended requests to God may be shortsighted when compared to His view. In such cases, we may be thankful that He does not grant them. To pray "In Jesus' name" acknowledges a dependence on His higher knowledge—as well as His higher power.

Focus on verses 15–31.

8. What all did Jesus mean when He said, "I will not leave you as orphans"? _____

_____

9. What can you know about the Holy Spirit from this passage? _____

_____

10. What aspect of the Spirit's work, as it is described here, do you particularly value? Why? _____

_____

11. How does the relationship between love and obedience help to answer Judas's question? _____

_____

12. Study verse 27. How does the peace Jesus spoke of here differ from the peace "the world gives"? _____

_____

13. Jesus said three times in this chapter that He will return. (See verses, 3, 18, and 28.) What effect does this promise have on you? _____

_____

14. a. When the disciples finally understood that they were about to lose Jesus, He began to comfort them with the words, "Do not let your hearts be troubled." What losses or potential losses trouble you? _____

_____

b. What truths could you draw from this chapter that might grant you stability during these periods of loss? _____

_____

_____

THIS WEEK

Jesus told his disciples, "In my Father's house are many rooms; . . . I am going there to prepare a place for you." If you belong to Jesus, He makes the same promise to you. Take time this week to explore your thoughts and feelings about heaven. Compose a painting, poem, or song that expresses some of these ideas. Use it as a prayer to Jesus.

19

YOU ARE MY FRIENDS

John 15:1–17

Judith Viorst in her book *Necessary Losses* enlarges our definition of friendship by listing six different categories of friends. There are convenience friends (the neighbor who carpools your kids), special-interest friends (your tennis group), historical friends (your best friend from grade school to whom you still write and see when you can), crossroads friends (your college roommate), cross-generational friends (the elderly lady in your church who is an extra grandma to you), and close friends (those few who share your secret thoughts and feelings, ones you could call at two in the morning). Friendship has many faces—and they all enrich our lives.

When Jesus looked for an example of love, an example His disciples could latch onto after He was gone, He chose friendship—and He used Himself as an illustration. True, a friendship with Jesus Christ (who is God) can never have the evenhanded give-and-take of healthy human friendships. (A friend of Jesus lets God be in charge.) Yet, in many other ways, Jesus showed, by His life—and death—what makes a good friend.

1. What do you value most in your relationship with a favorite friend? _____

_____

Read aloud John 15:1–17.

2. What can a branch of Christ's vine expect? _____

_____

3. In view of this picture of the vine and the branch, what can you know about the normal relationship between Jesus and His people? _____

_____

4. Circle each use of the word "remain" in your text and notice the different ways in which Jesus used that word. Why was it important that the disciples think this way about what it takes to "remain" at this point in their relationship to Jesus?

_____

_____

5. Study verse 8. If you were to show yourself to be Christ's disciple, what would you want people to see? _____

_____

Focus on verses 9–17.

6. What kinds of fruit does Jesus expect in the people who are attached to His vine? _____

_____

7. We will now look at this fruit in more detail. Why do you think that Jesus used the word "joy" instead of "happiness"? _____

_____

8. Why do you think Jesus used words like "obey" and "command" as a part of His farewell teaching? _____

_____

9. For the second and third time, in this final address, Jesus gives strong promises about prayer. (See John 14:14; 15:7; 15:16.) What influence would you like these statements to have on your own practice of prayer? _____

_____

10. Jesus stated twice here His new commandment of love, and He used His own love as an example. (Compare John 13:34–35 with John 15:12 and 17.) In what different ways throughout these events did Jesus show love to His disciples?

_____

11. How might these examples of Christ's love in action enrich your own relationships with other believers? _____

_____

12. What is the difference between a servant and a friend?

_____

13. Consider for a moment that Jesus says to you, "You _____ are my friend."
(your name)

After a moment to think, share with your group an answer to one of the questions below. How does this statement affect:

—your feelings about yourself? _____

_____

—your feelings about your work this week? _____

_____

—the purposes of your life? _____

_____

—what you would like to say to Jesus? _____

_____

—what you want to say about Jesus? _____

_____

—your relationships with His other friends? _____

_____

THIS WEEK

Write a letter to a friend. Tell your friend what you appreciate about him or her. Express thanksgiving for the gift of friendship that God has created between you.

20

THE WORLD WILL HATE YOU

John 15:18–16:16

"Hey, look at these roses, will you! See those spots? That's what you church people and your damn sprayers do to a man's yard." He was middle-aged, paunchy—and mad.

Our church member, on yard work duty for the month, continued spraying weeds in our trimmed grass, being careful to aim the spray away from neighboring yards—but the angry man railed on.

"And you and your noisy cars roaring in on Sunday morning kicking up dust. We can't even sleep around here. Christians! Blah!" And he spat.

We later paved our church parking lot to cut down dust, we built a buffer of trees and shrubs to protect adjoining yards, and we tried to be very careful about spraying. Years back, when we had built our church, farmland surrounded us, so we had to wonder why this particular neighbor had chosen to build his home next to a church parking lot. Was he mentally unbalanced? Was he just drunk the day he complained? Had we, in fact, damaged his roses? Or was he merely expressing an ordinary normal reaction of unbelievers toward Christians?

1. How do you think non-Christians see Christians in your community? _____

_____

2. Now change your point of view to different places. How do you think non-Christians see Christians in Japan, in the Middle East? In Mexico, in Russia, in South Africa? _____

_____

Read aloud John 15:18–16:4

3. What all did Jesus tell His followers to expect from those who do not believe in Him? _____

_____

4. What explanation did Jesus give for why His followers might not be well received in their world? _____

_____

5. Study more carefully verses 22–24. What danger does exposure to Jesus pose to an unbeliever? _____

_____

6. Study verses 26–27. In view of the reception Jesus anticipated for His followers, why do you think He still instructed them to testify about Him? _____

_____

7. Why do you think Jesus warned His disciples to expect hostility from the world? _____

_____

8. When have you sensed hostility from unbelievers because of your faith? _____

_____

9. a. Suppose you haven't noticed much hostility to your faith. No one persecutes you. No one has excommunicated you from a church or social group. As far as you know, no one hates you—except Uncle Harry, and he's supposed to be a Christian. In view of Christ's warning about the relationship between His followers and the world, how can you explain your current harmony? _____

_____

b. What can you be thankful for? _____

_____

c. What should you be concerned about? _____

_____

Read aloud John 16:5–16.
10. a. What is the Counselor's work in relation to the world? _____

_____

b. In relation to believers? _____

_____

c. In relation to Jesus? _____

_____

Look more carefully at verses 8–11.
11. Of what value is it to an unbeliever to be convicted of sin, righteousness, and judgment? _____

_____

12. In various translations of this passage, the Holy Spirit is called the Counselor, the Comforter, the Helper, the Advocate, the Spirit of Truth. How do each of these names help explain His character? _____

_____

13. When have you particularly appreciated the work of God the Holy Spirit? _____

_____

THIS WEEK

Many Christians around the world experience severe suffering because of their faith in Jesus. This week write a letter to one of these brothers or sisters. Or write to an authority in an oppressive government, or to one of your own political leaders who might exercise influence to improve human rights around the world.

One source of more specific information is Slavic Gospel Association, 129 North Washington, Wheaton, Illinois 60187.

21

I HAVE OVERCOME THE WORLD

John 16:16–33

My friends' sixteen-year-old daughter had died. It was a sudden death—unanticipated and, to this day, unexplained. One Sunday morning their healthy sixteen-year-old simply stopped breathing—and died.

I sat that day with them around their dining room table. We picked at fresh fruit from a large wooden bowl brought by a thoughtful friend. The doorbell and phone rang constantly, giving some purpose to my presence, a feeble busyness against an ocean of grief.

We held each other and cried. But oddly, we didn't cry all the time. Instead, we talked about the mechanics of the next few days: canceled appointments, trips to the airport, food and beds. We remembered together funny things their daughter had done and said. Sometimes we even laughed.

The funeral service, when it came, was a similar mixture of grief and joy. When the choir sang, "Children of the

Heavenly Father,'' I cried. Yet when the speaker shouted in triumph the Scripture's promise of resurrection and new life, I rejoiced. Not that this joy erases grief. Even ten years later as my friends speak of their daughter's death, he puts his arm around his wife as if to ward off the continuing hurt.

Jesus recognized this mixture of grief and joy in the face of death—and talked with His disciples about it. He was about to die—and His friends would grieve. Yet, He was about to conquer death, not only His own death, but theirs as well. Because of Jesus, even our deepest grief is framed with joy.

1. a. If you were to compose a painting of joy, what would you paint? _____

_____

b. How would you paint grief? _____

_____

Read aloud John 16:16–24.

2. What were the disciples worried about? _____

_____

3. a. Circle in your Bible each reference to mourning or joy. In what ways are the two related? _____

_____

b. Will grief or joy be stronger for Christ's followers? Why? _____

_____

4. Tell about your feelings when you first saw your first baby—or when a friend gave birth to her first child. _____

_____

5. How would Christ's illustration of labor and birth help the disciples understand what they would experience in the next few days? _____

_____

6. What kinds of praying did Jesus encourage in verses 23–24? _____

_____

7. If you were to put these prayer concepts into practice, what would you talk to God about? _____

_____

8. Once again, Jesus made clear that we must pray in His name. What beliefs and actions does a prayer in Christ's name imply? _____

_____

Read aloud John 16:25–33.

9. a. What reasons did the disciples have here to feel encouraged? _____

_____

b. What reasons did they have to feel discouraged? _____

_____

10. Look more carefully at verses 29–32. What strengths and weaknesses do you see in the disciples' faith? _____

_____

11. In what ways do you see a similar mixture of belief and unbelief in your own faith? _____

_____

12. Look back at the way Jesus described "the world" in John 15:18–16:4. What do you think Jesus meant when He said, "I have overcome the world"? _____

_____

13. In view of the grief that Jesus had warned His disciples they were about to experience, why might they find joy in His statements of verse 33? _____

_____

14. In your own current setting, how might the words of verse 33 reassure you? _____

_____

THIS WEEK

Can you think of someone who especially needs to hear the message of John 16:33? Write a letter to that person this week. Use this verse as a foundation for encouragement.

22

JESUS PRAYS—FOR ME

John 17

I hadn't felt well for months. A chronic stomach problem had flared up and boiled over. A variety of prescribed medications hadn't helped. I felt sick if I ate and sick if I didn't. My weight, always low, dropped to the eighties. Climbing a flight of stairs was hard work.

I nibbled the corner of a saltine from my desk drawer and tried to construct healthy sentences across yellow work sheets, but my brain felt as puny as my body. After a couple of hours, I gave up and headed out of my borrowed office in Wheaton's Billy Graham Center and wandered through the museum, hoping to clear my head. Eventually, I wound up in a small prayer chapel.

There, I talked to God, not about my work, or my soul, but about my stomach. I was tired of picking over full supper plates—and leaving them full. I was tired of needing to know where the bathroom was in every building I entered—in case what little I'd eaten didn't stay. And I was bone tired of feeling nauseated every waking minute. I don't know exactly what I said to God. Nothing eloquent, mostly a squeaked, "Help."

I had barely said, "Amen," when I heard a familiar voice in the hall: Rosemary. Rosemary lived forty miles distant, and I hadn't seen her for six months. But here she was as if on cue from God. Rosemary, my friend, is also a doctor.

It didn't take her long to assess the situation. Over lunch (thin soup and crackers), she gave me the most practical medical advice I'd had so far. She also insisted that I see a specialist. Then she presented the best gift of all, "I will pray for you every day, about your stomach."

And she did. I didn't get well overnight. But from that point, I began to improve. Even on the bad days, just knowing that Rosemary cared and Rosemary prayed to our God—for me—brought me courage.

Jesus gave His disciples a similar gift. But He didn't limit His gift of prayer to His first-century disciples. He also prays for us—you and me.

1. a. When have you appreciated someone else's praying? Tell about it. _____

_____

b. What did your parents teach you about prayer? _____

_____

Read aloud Christ's prayer for Himself, John 17:1–5.

2. What had Jesus done that gave a sense of completion to His work? _____

_____

3. Jesus used some form of the word "glory" five times in this section of His prayer. What relationship can you see between the death Jesus was about to experience and "glory" as He described it here? _____

_____

Read aloud Christ's prayer for His disciples, John 17:6–19.

4. As you slowly read this prayer, use the space below to draw a picture of the relationship between Jesus, His Father, and His disciples. Begin by putting your pencil on Jesus. Without lifting your pencil, draw a line from one to the other each time they appear in the text.

Jesus

Father   Disciples

What impresses you about the way Jesus, His Father, and His disciples relate to each other? _____

_____

5. What factors did you notice that connect Jesus, His disciples, and His Father to each other? _____

_____

6. Jesus prayed that His disciples would become "one" just as He and His Father are one (verse 11). What dimensions would you expect this kind of unity to take among Christ's disciples? _____

_____

7. Jesus spoke three times of protection for His disciples (verses 11, 12, and 15). What tensions needing protection did Jesus seem to expect that His disciples would face? _____

_____

8. a. Study more carefully verses 13–19 by marking each use of the word "world." "Sanctify" (verse 17) means "set apart." In what ways were the disciples to be in the world, yet set apart from it? _____

_____

b. What do you think is hard about that position? _____

_____

9. How might the unity described throughout this prayer help Christ's disciples live out their difficult role in the world?

_____

_____

Read aloud Christ's prayer for future believers, John 17:20–26.

10. Circle words in this prayer that express unity. What feelings does the possibility of your own unity with the Father, Jesus, and His first-generation disciples raise in your mind? Explain. _____

_____

11. What reasons did Jesus give for bringing future believers into this unity? (See verses 21, 22, 24, 26.) _____

_____

12. a. If you were to rate yourself on how well you are fulfilling the purposes you discussed in question 11, what letter grade would you give yourself? _____

_____

b. What could you do that would improve the grade you gave yourself? _____

_____ _____

13. If you were facing a hard day (or year), what encouragement would this prayer offer you? _____

_____

THIS WEEK

Select a person to whom you are united by faith in Jesus. This week pray every day for that person. If your friend has special needs, consider making a covenant to pray daily for him or her for a set period of time. Tell your friend of this promise.

23

BETRAYED AND DENIED—BY FRIENDS

John 18:1–27

I have only been hysterical once (so far) in my life. But I picked an inconvenient time for it. It was winter, a cold January. I was "due any day" for baby number two. Our furnace had malfunctioned. After more than a week without heat, we had finally found the right replacement furnace for the right price. My husband and a friend had spent a Saturday installing the new furnace. While baby number one (now almost two years old) played quietly in her bedroom, Roger called me downstairs to admire his day of work while he turned on the welcome warmth.

Suddenly, we heard a screeching thud from upstairs followed by shrieks of pain. We tore upstairs to find Sheri screaming on the floor near an overturned rocking chair and smearing her face with a bloody hand. Shaking all over, I picked her up, discovered the ends of two fingers missing— and went crazy. My husband had to call friends to help him take care of us both.

It all ended reasonably well. Sheri's fingers healed smoothly enough for her to become a musician. I delivered a healthy baby girl the next morning. I also learned a little about my own limitations. Calm, steady, reliable me—isn't always that way.

1. a. When has your own reaction to a crisis surprised you?

_____

_____

b. What did you learn about yourself in that situation? __

_____

2. In his story of Jesus, John often painted Peter and Judas side by side. Review John's picture of these two major characters by dividing your group into two sections. For ten or fifteen minutes let one section study Peter and the other study Judas. (You will often use the same passage.) Then summarize your findings to the whole group.

PETER

a. How did Peter begin to follow Jesus? (John 1:35—44) __

_____

b. What insight and courage did Peter show? (John 6:66—69) _____

_____

c. What did Peter's reaction at Christ's foot-washing ceremony reveal about his character? (John 13:1—11) _____

_____

d. Why do you think Peter asked the question of verse 24? (John 13:21—30) _____

_____

e. What did Peter know and not know about himself? (John 13:33–38) _____

_____

JUDAS

a. What did Jesus know about Judas? (John 6:66–71) ___

_____

b. How did Judas's view of money differ from Mary's? (John 12:1–6) _____

_____

c. Do you think that Jesus washed Judas's feet? If so, what can you imagine that each of them was thinking at the time? (John 13:1–11) _____

_____

d. Why do the words "And it was night" seem an appropriate way to end this episode? (John 13:18–30) _____

_____

3. a. Peter and Judas were with each other during many of the events you just read about. How do you think they felt about each other? _____

_____

b. What do their differing responses suggest about their belief or lack of belief in Jesus? _____

_____

Read aloud John 18:1–11.

4. a. If you were painting a picture of what happened here, which phase would you select? _____

_____

b. What would you include in your painting? _____

_____

Note: Do you wonder what happened to Malchus, the wounded servant? See Luke 22:51.

5. Do you consider Jesus active or passive in these scenes? Why? _____

_____

6. Why do you think Jesus did not use the intervening hours, since He had last seen Judas, to escape? (Review also John 10:14–18.) _____

_____

7. What effect do you think these events had on Peter? On Judas? _____

_____

Read aloud John 18:12–27.

8. Why do you think the high priest asked Jesus about His disciples and His teaching? _____

_____

Note: Who was Annas? "Annas, the father-in-law of Caiaphas, had been high priest between the years 7 and 14. Following him at intervals, five of his sons and his son-in-law held the office. He wielded a powerful influence, and was regarded as high priest emeritus" (Tenney, page 256).

9. a. While Jesus endured questioning inside, Peter was being questioned outside. Why do you think Peter was there?

_____

_____

b. Who all spoke to Peter and with what intent? _____

_____

10. If you had been Peter, what thoughts would have rushed to your mind when you heard the rooster crow? _____

_____

11. If you had been the other disciple (perhaps John) at Peter's side, what would you have said to him? _____

_____

The story of Peter is not over—but the Judas story is. Read aloud Matthew 27:1–5.

12. Why might you expect Peter to express his remorse in a different way than Judas did? _____

_____

13. How could belief in Jesus help you recover from your own failures? _____

_____

THIS WEEK

Examine your faith in Jesus this week. Ask yourself some of these questions:

Do I believe in Jesus only because it is convenient, because my family and friends expect me to believe? Or would I choose to believe in Jesus, even in hostile circumstances?

To what extent do I believe in Jesus? Do I believe merely that Jesus was a good man with good teachings? Or do I believe that Jesus is God, who came to earth in human form?

Do I believe that Jesus died because evil men chose to kill Him? Or do I believe that Jesus willingly chose to die—for me?

Do I believe that only those people who have committed terrible wrongs need to come to Jesus and be changed? Or do I believe that Jesus died to pay for my own sins, the small ones as well as the large?

Do I believe that I should turn to Jesus in a crisis, but that I can manage most of my life myself? Or do I believe that all that I am and all that I do belong first to Jesus?

This week, try every day to express your belief in Jesus—to Him in prayer, and (by action or word) to some other person.

24

WHAT IS TRUTH?

John 18:28–19:42

"What is truth? said jesting Pilate; and would not stay for an answer," wrote Francis Bacon in 1625 as he opened his essay "Of Truth."

We, too, look for truth—sometimes in a cat-and-mouse game with God. (Come and find where I'm hiding, God. Then I'll believe.) Sometimes in a search for spiritual thrill. (Make me tingle and see stars, God, so that I can believe.) Sometimes in painful desperation. (I can't survive without You, God. I must believe.) And sometimes in a quiet choice. (I can't prove You are there, God, but evidence points in that direction; I choose to believe.)

Others look for less religious paths to truth: money, relationships, power, booze, knowledge, sex, psychotherapy. Do they find it? Perhaps they grasp a corner of truth now and then—enough to whet the appetite for some gigantic absolute, somewhere out there: the Eternal. God reveals

Himself in myriad ways, and some of the most contrary avenues may, at His direction, circle back toward Him.

Yet, for eternal truth, we must somehow encounter Jesus, Himself. As Jesus said to the questioning Thomas in John 14:6–7, "I am the way, and the truth, and the life. No one comes to the Father except through me."

At one point, Pilate may have tried, at least halfheartedly, to find that Truth. It was when Jesus Christ stood before Him—for trial.

1. Review the questions in the previous activity called *This Week*. What do these reveal about your own concept of truth? _____

_____

Note: Pilate was the Roman governor of Judea. Since the Roman government did not allow Jewish religious courts to execute people, the Jews who wanted Jesus killed took Him to Pilate for trial.

Read aloud John 18:28–19:22.

2. How would you describe the general tone of the conversation between Pilate and the Jews who brought Jesus to him? _____

_____

3. Find each time that Pilate went in or out of his palace. What does this suggest about his methods for conducting this trial? _____

_____

4. Study Pilate's conversations with the Jewish accusers. In what ways did Pilate and the Jews seem to move at cross-purposes? _____

_____

5. Study the conversations between Pilate and Jesus in John 18:33–38 and 19:8–11. If Pilate had been "on the side of truth," what could he have learned here? _____

_____

6. What mixture of justice and cruelty do you find in Pilate? _____

_____

7. Verse 8 says that Pilate was "even more afraid." What reasons throughout this event did Pilate have to be frightened? _____

_____

8. In what different ways did Pilate try to avoid ruling on this case? _____

_____

9. Pilate stated three times that he could find no evidence of Christ's guilt (John 18:38; 19:4; 19:6). In view of this, why do you think Pilate permitted the execution? _____

_____

10. Notice each time this passage mentions the idea of Jesus as King. In view of these, why do you think Pilate placed the sign on the cross, "JESUS OF NAZARETH, THE KING OF THE JEWS"? _____

_____

11. Study Pilate's question of John 18:38, "What is truth?" Do you think Pilate really wanted to know the answer?

Explain. _____

_____

Read aloud John 19:23–42.

   12. a. What cruelty do you see in Christ's death? _____

_____

      b. What mercy? _____

_____

Note: Why did Roman soldiers break the legs of those being crucified? Crucifixion was a slow, cruel death, taking up to three days to do its job. Each breath required the person to put weight on his pierced feet in order to fill his lungs. Thus, breaking the legs brought a faster end. Jesus was spared this final indignity—in order to fulfill Scripture. Even so, the soldier's sword made sure He was dead.

   13. Joseph and Nicodemus were both wealthy religious Jews. What conflicts and risks did they face?_____

_____

   14. Glance back at John 3:1–21 and 7:50–52 to review your introduction to Nicodemus. What changes in Nicodemus do you think brought him to this point? _____

_____

   15. John once more refers to truth in 19:35 where he says that he has testified of these events "so that you also may believe." How does Christ's death fit into your own beliefs about Jesus? _____

_____

THIS WEEK

You are drawing near the end of your study of John's gospel. This week, page back through the gospel of John and your study guide. Make notes on ideas, teachings, conversations in your group that you would like to see as lasting influences on your faith. Then present these notes to God in prayer. Ask Him to nurture you through this study of His Book.

25

THAT YOU MAY BELIEVE

John 20

"He hung the key by the back door," said *someone* about the writer, John. I've tried in vain to chase down the author of the quote. Alas, I've fallen prey to one of the many traps for writers: I took inadequate notes. Somewhere early in this project, I spotted that gem—only then it didn't seem so significant. Since then, I've seen over and over the unspoken theme of John's gospel painted in a dozen ways: I'm telling you this so that you may believe. And sure enough, as I came to the final chapters, I found the key by the back door.

There, John describes his own mission, his reason for writing the book. As if he were an artist finished with his painting and signing his name in the lower right corner, John writes, "Jesus did many other miraculous signs in the presence of his disciples, which are not recorded in this book. But these are written that you may believe that Jesus is the Christ, the Son of God, and that by believing you may have life in his name."

As you approach these final chapters, take note of what John wanted you to believe—and why. Then let his record of Jesus test your beliefs.

Read aloud John 20.

1. What different moods or emotions do you sense in this story? _____

_____

2. Take note of each character. What purpose do you see for his or her being included in this account? _____

_____

3. a. If you had had the benefit of looking over the shoulders of Mary and Peter during the events of the past three days, what evidences would you have seen that Jesus had died and was alive again? (Begin at John 19:31 and find all that you can.) _____

_____

b. To what extent are you convinced by these events? ___

_____

4. How would the Christian faith be different if it did not hold to a resurrected Jesus? (Consider purpose of life, view of death, view of afterlife, nature of Jesus, and purpose of His death.) _____

_____

Look again at Mary as you study verses 10–18.

5. a. What changes in Mary's belief do you see from the beginning to the end of this section? _____

_____

b. What different emotions accompanied these beliefs?

_____

c. In what different ways did God show His love for Mary? _____

_____

Look again at verses 19–23.

6. What obstacles do you think the disciples had to overcome in order to meet together? _____

_____

7. Study Christ's words to His disciples. How might His message to them create "peace"? _____

_____

Look again at verses 24–29.

8. What common ground do you find with Thomas? _____

_____

9. How does the conversation between Thomas and Jesus help you with your own doubts? _____

_____

Study verses 30–31, the "key" to the book of John.

10. What did John want his readers to believe? Why? _____

_____

11. How has John's gospel helped you to know Jesus? Begin your answers with, "Jesus is . . . ," then cite an event or teaching from John's gospel that reveals this quality in Jesus. _____

_____

12. Verse 31 says, "But these are written that you may believe. . . ." How might your study of John help you through a time when it is hard for you to believe? _____

_____

THIS WEEK

This week plant a bulb in a special place in your yard, or in a pot in your house. As it grows into life, a life already possessed in the interior of the bulb, let it remind you of Jesus raised from the dead—and of your own life in Him.

26

DO YOU LOVE ME MORE THAN THESE?

John 21

Right now, I'm in a position many mothers envy. Two of our children still live at home. Two others (one married) are grown and live nearby. A mere picking up the phone and, with a few scheduling gymnastics, I can have our whole family of seven seated for dinner at our dining room table.

To cut down on scheduling hassles, we simply schedule dinner—on Sundays at 1:30. After dinner, we sprawl in front of the living room fire, prop ourselves up to watch TV football, or, depending on the season, ease outdoors with Frisbees and skateboards. Sometimes we break up into twos and threes to read, talk, play a game, do dishes, knit, but we're still together. It is a family day. I even bought a new dining room table (expandable to twelve) in honor of this time of family unity.

Soon, too soon, my enviable position as housemother will end. Graduate school and jobs will take our children, one by one, to other parts of the country. Our family times at the expandable dining room table may come only once or twice a year. Yet even then, I think these memories of Sunday after Sunday together will come back and add their weight of value to the less frequent visits.

We can't ever re-create this stage of our family—but we can build on it. So I hope that twenty years from now, today's Sunday dinner at home will, by memory, continue to nurture family love.

1. What family events have you experienced that drew you together? _____

_____

Read aloud John 21:1–14.

2. Why do you think these seven disciples went back to Galilee? _____

_____

3. Three of the men, Peter, Thomas, and John, figured prominently in the past two chapters. If you had been one of them, what might you have been thinking during that long night in the boat? _____

_____

4. Why do you think Peter jumped into the sea? _____

_____

5. What actions served to remind these men of their past experiences with Jesus? _____

_____

6. What changes of emotions would you expect in these men between verses 3 and 14? _____

_____

Read aloud John 21:15–25.

7. How might the events of the recent past influence the kind of love Peter thought he could commit to Jesus? _____

_____

8. When Jesus asked Peter, ". . . do you truly love me more than these?" what might Jesus have meant by "these"? _____

_____

9. Why do you think Jesus asked Peter three times if he loved Him? _____

_____

10. What job description did Jesus give Peter? (Look in each of verses 15 through 19.) _____

_____

11. Why do you think Jesus said to Peter, "Follow Me"? __

_____

12. What effect do you think this job description would have on Peter? _____

_____

13. a. What influence would the events of this chapter have on the feelings of these men concerning the future return of Jesus mentioned in verse 22? _____

_____

b. How do the events in this chapter affect your own feelings about that return? _____

_____

14. John, inspired by God, wrote these twenty-one chapters of the gospel that bears his name. In view of verses 22–

25, what did John see as his job and purpose? _____

_____

15. After three years together, Jesus asked Peter three times, "Do you love me?" Do you, like Peter, love Jesus more now than when you began your study of John? Explain. _

_____

THIS WEEK

Write a love letter to Jesus. Use it as a prayer.

HELPS FOR LEADERS

1 / THE WORD BECAME FLESH

John 1:1–34

1. Encourage brief, one-phrase answers from as many different group members as possible.

2. Your group should find answers to part a. in nearly every verse.

6. Invite emotional as well as intellectual responses to this passage thus far.

7. Use this question to outline the events described here. A good response might begin, "I see . . . "

9. See verses 6–8, 15, 19, 23, 26–27, 29–31, 34. A question may arise regarding John's answer to the priests and Levites in verse 21. In Matthew 11:14, Jesus declared that John indeed fulfilled the role of Elijah that Malachi 3:1 had promised. Perhaps these Jewish leaders looked for Elijah's reincarnation. That, John declared, he was not.

10. Compare the information in verses 29–34 with that in verses 19–28.

2 / FOLLOW ME

John 1:35–2:25

1. Note: The unnamed other disciple of John the Baptist mentioned in verses 35–37 may have been John, the writer of this gospel.

3. If it seems appropriate, treat these two questions together.

4. See verses 36, 41, 45, and 49.

5. Because Jesus was both—fully God and fully man—He could open heaven to all who receive Him. Perhaps the ascending and descending angels symbolize the free movement between heaven and earth: God to earth, His people to heaven.

11. The temple that Jesus referred to was, of course, His own body. While the Jews were busy calculating the size of building stones and construction time, Jesus was speaking of His own redeeming death and His resurrection (in three days), when He would not only exercise authority over all of sin but also over death, thereby granting eternal life to all who follow Him.

3 / BORN AGAIN

John 3

4. See verses 3, 5, 7, and 15.

6. See verses 10–15.

7. a. Consider similarities in problem, purpose, and actual event. (The snake on a pole was much like Jesus on the cross.)

b. Your group should discuss the possible effect of this story on Nicodemus after he had witnessed or heard of Christ's crucifixion. For a biblical record of Nicodemus at a later time, look ahead to John 7:50 and 19:39.

8. Focus on verse 18.

11–12. Optional questions.

13. Your group should note John's deference to Jesus— even at his own expense. It should also note the similarity between verses 18 and 36.

14. Relevant responses appear in verses 3, 5, 7, 13–15, 16, and most especially in verses 18 and 36.

4 / I AM THE CHRIST

John 4:1–42

4. a. Regarding the position that Jesus took in the Jew/Samaritan conflict, verses 21–24 spell it out. He did say a point blank, "Salvation is from the Jews." Yet, verses 21 and 23 suggest a coming change in the place and form of worship.

b. Study verses 21–24.

10. b. The "four months" of verse 35 is an interesting allusion to the normal time lapse between planting and harvest in agriculture. But here the sower (Jesus) and reapers (the woman and the disciples) can rejoice together because the time lapse between hearing the gospel and receiving it as truth is so short.

11. See verses 39–42.

12. Be sure your group states each identity in these five verses correctly, since they form the basis for the final part of today's discussion.

13. Assume that not everyone will have already arrived at Christ's "Savior of the world" identity. After all, Sychar gave an unusually fast harvest. Adopt an attitude that invites an honest response, not necessarily a "correct" answer. Then use the second part of the question to encourage spiritual growth from any current position.

5 / BARRIERS TO BELIEF

John 4:43–5:15

Note: The whole gospel of John records only seven "signs and wonders" (miracles). Today's study composes two of them.

1. See John 2:1–11 and 13–25 to review the previous events cited here. Note: Cana was only ten miles from Nazareth, where Jesus grew up.

5. If your group is slow to spot the father's dilemma, ask, "If you had been that father, why might you have hesitated before turning towards home?" Compare the father's actions with verse 48.

7. Draw information from verses 47, 48, 50, 51, 52, and 53.

11. See verses 5, 7, and 9.

14. Your group should suggest several endings to the sentence. Among them, "Jesus is Master over time, space, and Sabbath."

15. Barriers suggested by the text include: rebellion against what is close (4:44), desire for miracles—or gifts from God (4:48), lack of desire to "get well"—or grow (5:6), trusting other avenues of help (5:7), overconcern for rules (5:10), unwillingness to abandon favorite sins (5:14).

6 / FROM DEATH TO LIFE

John 5:16–47

2. Your group should find some six connections along with a couple of subpoints.

3. See verse 23.

4. See verse 20.

5. Spot answers in verses 20, 21, 22, and 23.

6. See verses 25 and 28.

7. See verses 24 and 29.

8. Verse 30 sets the specific context for Christ's statement, but His argument throughout has led to this point.

9. Your group should find four separate witnesses in these verses:

John (the Baptist), verses 32–35

Christ's works, verse 36

God the Father, verses 37–38

Scripture, verses 39–40

13. This is an optional question.

14. a. See verses 21 and 24.

b. See verses 21 and 26.

c. See verses 21, 24, and 29.

7 / FIVE THOUSAND FOR LUNCH!

John 6:1–24

3. See verses 1 and 2. Motives may also grow from the events of the previous chapter.

4. This is a fairly common point of view. It is hard to square, however, with the words of verses 13 and 14. Your group should also notice the reaction of the crowd—a safe barometer in most accounts. Would they have behaved in such a way after a mere exercise in sharing?

5. This miracle of multiplying the loaves and fish was really an act of creation—not at all difficult for the triune God of Genesis 1 who said, "Let *us* make man in our image."

9. See verses 16, 19, 22. Notice the distance of the disciples from shore, the response of the disciples, and the response of the crowd.

11. See verses 22–24.

12. Your group should review the close tie between Jesus and His Father, described throughout John 5. John 6 exhibits the creative power of God—yet Jesus, the Son, does the work. Perhaps the miracles were meant to visualize His unity with the Father as taught in John 5.

8 / BREAD OF LIFE

John 6:25–71

4. See verses 29, 35, and 40.

5. See verses 36–39. Verses 44–45, 64–65, and 70–71 give additional information.

7. Be sure that your group has now disengaged itself from the error of Christ's first-century hearers: the idea of literal bread, physical hunger, and physical thirst.

8. See verses 41–42 and 52.

11. See verse 54.

13. a. Perhaps the one most likely offense to these devout Jews was the suggestion that they should drink His blood (verse 53). Christ's repeated claim to close ties with the Father God (verses 45–51) might also prove highly offensive to monotheistic Jews.

b. Some participants, with twentieth-century hindsight, may find nothing but joy and comfort here. Others, particularly those who are not yet full believers, may find some alarming concepts. Now is a good time to express them.

14. a. See verses 64–65, 70–71.

b. See verses 62–63, 65, 68–69.

15. For those who decided to follow Christ in childhood ask, "Did you decide to keep on following Jesus once you were grown up? Why?"

9 / LIVING WATER

John 7

3. Your group should spot four effects in verses 10–13 as well as two major divisions among the people.

4. Encourage a little creative role play here. Possible positions include (1) Where is He? (2) He is good. (3) He deceives the people. (4) Fear.

5. a. See verses 14, 16, 19, 23, 28–29, and 37.

b. Clues from the passage include verses 31 and 33.

c. See verses 19, 20, 25, and 32.

6. a. Compare verses 15–19 with verse 20.

b. Use all of verses 14–24.

c. Compare verses 3–6 with verse 18.

7. a. See verses 27 and 41–42. Questions about origin have already come up in verses 3–5, 14–15, and 20.

b. See especially verses 28–29. As for the question of verses 41–44, Jesus did, of course, live in Galilee, but He was born in Bethlehem of David's lineage. (See the early chapters of either Matthew or Luke.)

8. a. See verses 6–8, 33–34.

10 / LIGHT OF THE WORLD

John 8:1–30

1. Try to involve each person in your group with this question. Be sure that the range of emotions covers all stages of the event.

2. Your group may suggest any number of answers. The behavior of these accusers raises many questions. For example,

Was the situation a set-up—with the woman and Jesus both victims?

Did her partner escape, or was he allowed to flee?

Did the religious leaders value the woman less than her male partner—or did they blame her more?

4. If you want an extra question, ask, "What do you think Jesus wrote on the ground?"

7. Someone should point out the question of verse 19, a probable slur about Christ's paternity. Did the conditions of His birth cause Jesus to be viewed as a bastard?

11 / WHO DO YOU THINK YOU ARE?

John 8:31−59

1. See verses 31−32.

3. If responses are slow, break down the question into parts by asking, What did Jesus mean by "freedom"? By "slavery"? What did the Jews mean by those terms?

4. Discuss "ordinary" sins as well as the larger ones.

5. See verses 39−41.

6. a. See verses 37−41.

b. See verses 40, 41, 42, 44, and 46.

7. Use information from verses 31−32, 35, 36, 42, and 47.

8. Compare verse 31 with verse 47.

12. "I am" is an assertion of absolute timeless existence (Tenney, p. 150). The Jews did not misunderstand Christ's claim to deity.

13. Some passages (not all quotes from Jesus) include: John 1:1−3; 1:14; 1:24; 1:29; 1:41; 1:49; 3:16; 4:25−26; 4:42; 6:35; 6:51; 6:68; 7:37−38; 8:12; 8:16; 8:42; 8:58.

12 / I WAS BLIND BUT NOW I SEE!

John 9

2. Your group should point out several helpful aspects of Christ's work here. Among them: A man had been a public beggar, so Jesus healed him publicly.

Jesus employed the man's sense of touch and hearing—those senses most familiar to him.

Jesus sent him away to wash—thus affirming his independence.

Jesus allowed him to act in faith. (The blind man had no

evidence that he could see until he left Jesus and washed in the pool.)

4. a. See verses 1–2.

b. See verses 8–12.

c. See verses 18–23.

d. See verses 13–34.

e. See verses 3–7 and 35–38.

7. Your group should look at verses 11, 17, 30–33, 36, and 38. Help people go beyond a mere quoting of the blind man's words to an interpretation of what these words reveal of his faith at that point.

11. Compare verse 11 with verse 35.

13 / THE GOOD SHEPHERD

John 10

1. Jesus listed some seventeen actions on characteristics in this brief allegory.

5. Your group should point out the stranger of verse 5, the thieves and robbers of verses 1 and 8–10, the hired hand (perhaps a symbol of Jewish religious leaders) in verses 12–13, and the wolf in the same verses.

8. See verses 19–21 and preceding verses for reasons.

12. a. See verse 24.

b. Find responses throughout verses 25–39.

13. See verses 26 and 33 as well as inferences throughout the passage.

Note on verses 34–36: Merrill Tenney in *John: The Gospel of Belief* interprets this enigmatic passage as follows: "If the Scripture (Ps. 82:6), 'which cannot be broken,' applied the term "gods" to ordinary men, should not the term "Son of

God" be allowable to Him whom the Father had set apart specially and sent into the world for an unusual mission?" (p. 169)

14 / LAZARUS, COME FORTH!

John 11

2. a. See verses 2–3, 5–6, and 11.
b. See verses 7–8 and 13–16.
3. See verses 4 and 11–14.
4. Clues appear in verses 4 and 14–15, each introduced by the phrase "so that."
5. These statements of regret appear in verses 21–22, 32, and 37. If you need a clarifying question, try, "What were they believing about Jesus, and what were they wondering about?"
6. See verses 23–27 and 33–36.
11. Compare the response of people in verse 45 with that spoken of in verse 46 and following.
12. a. Interpret verses 48–49.
b. Interpret verses 49–52. God used Caiaphas (probably because of his God-ordained office of high priest) to interpret God's actions of the present and to predict the future. Caiaphas probably thought it was better for Jesus (one man) to die than for the whole nation of Jews, visiting Jerusalem for Passover, to spark war with Roman soldiers. But God used those words, which John recorded here, for a larger spiritual meaning.

15 / HOSANNA!

John 12:1–19

4. Draw information from verses 1, 4, 7, 9–10.

5. Consider their views of money, their views of themselves, their views of Jesus, their perceptions of the future.

6. Don't be surprised if some group members say they would have seen Mary's actions as embarrassing and overdone, while Judas's words as practical and farsighted. Not everyone present at the table with him would have known that Judas was a thief—and that he would soon betray Jesus.

7. This was a special situation. Jesus knew that His death was only days away. Those who wanted to show their love for Him had only a short time to do so. They could care for the poor a couple of weeks later.

10. See the actions of Martha (verse 2), Mary (verse 3), the crowd (verse 13), the disciples (verse 16).

12. Your group will find several correlations in this psalm. Key words include: "gates" (verse 19), "salvation" (verse 21), "stone" (verse 22), "builders rejected" (verse 22), "capstone" (verse 22), and others.

16 / FATHER, GLORIFY YOUR NAME

John 12:20–50

2. Forms of the word "glorified" appear in verses 23, 28, and 41. Jesus speaks of some form of His glory throughout verses 23–36.

4. Use this question to continue your study of verses 23–32.

5. Study verses 34–36 with this question.

8. See verses 27–28 and related issues.

10. Does God deliberately blind some people to Jesus? It would push the passage here too far to say that God brings about unbelief. Instead, we should see it as a strong warning that our own initial unbelief may bring on serious consequences regarding our ability to believe at a later time. The message God has sent—and our own reaction to it—can blind our eyes and deaden our hearts.

11. See verses 42 and following as well as the previous warning of verse 25. The "closet Christian" approach may have been a tempting solution to people who faced the choices you discussed in question 6. Jesus says here that this kind of "belief" won't work. As reasons, He cites His own connection with the Father—and coming judgment.

17 / LOVE ONE ANOTHER

John 13

2. Read this question to your group *before* you read the passage aloud so that people can watch for ways Jesus showed love. Your group should discover aspects of Christ's love in verses 4–5, 7, 15, 17, 19, 33, 36, 38.

Other demonstrations of Christ's love hinge on this chapter, though they are not addressed outright. For example, why did Jesus tell Judas, "What you are about to do, do quickly"? A comparison with John 12:10 shows that the life of Lazarus was in danger. Perhaps Jesus prolonged Lazarus's life by hastening His own death.

4. If after a few minutes of discussion no one has pointed out verse 16, direct attention to it and ask, "How is the relationship between the Father, Jesus, and His disciples further clarified by Jesus washing His disciples' feet?''

18 / I WILL NOT LEAVE YOU ORPHANS

John 14

4. Some group members may resent Jesus' claim to be the exclusive route to the Father. A few may reject it outright. (How could God condemn an honest Muslim—just because he doesn't know Jesus?) But in spite of these objections, your group should notice that John does indeed record these as the words of Jesus. Those who accept these words will likely express feelings of concern and responsibility for the world's non-Christians.

7. Use this question to study verses 12–14.

8. Draw answers from all of verses 15–31.

9. Draw answers from verses 16, 17, and 26.

11. Study verses 22–24.

12. In order to answer this question, your group will need to first discuss the kind of peace the world gives (absence of war, economic security, guilt-free sex). How is the peace Jesus offers different from this?

19 / YOU ARE MY FRIENDS

John 15:1–17

2. Your group should find about six expectations in verses 1–6.

6. Several kinds of fruit appear throughout these verses.

Among them, your group should notice: joy (verse 11), obedience (verses 10 and 14), love (verses 12–13 and 17), effective prayer (verses 7 and 16).

7. See verse 11.

8. See verses 10 and 12–14.

10. Your group should find answers throughout verses 9–17. Among these, people should notice the following: Jesus set an example of obedience to the Father (verse 10), He will lay down His life (verse 13), He calls them friends (verse 14), He shared with them the knowledge the Father had given to Him (verse 15), He chose them (verse 16), He gives them a purpose—to bear lasting fruit (verse 16).

20 / THE WORLD WILL HATE YOU

John 15:18–16:16

4. Use this question to study all of verses 18–25. Merrill Tenney found in these verses three major reasons for hostility between Christians and the world. (1) Christians are of a different nature from unbelievers (verse 19). (2) Christians are closely related to Jesus—whom the world also hates and would soon kill (verses 18, 20, 21, 25). (3) Christians remind unbelievers of their sin (verses 22–24).

5. Exposure to Jesus and His message forces a choice. One must thereafter respond either positively or negatively. And those who reject Jesus do so with an increased awareness of their own sin—and therefore increased guilt.

7. See John 16:1 and 4.

9. In a culture where Christianity is popular, Christians may not experience the harsh treatment Jesus predicted. These Christians enjoy the blessings and protection of a vast company of fellow believers and a culture that, to some extent, follows the teachings of Jesus. For this, they can thank God.

But such benign environment carries its own risks. These protected people must ask:

Am I a true believer in Jesus—or am I just following the path of least resistance?

Am I actively looking for points of tension between Christ's teachings and popular opinion so that I will remain faithful even in these pressured areas?

Am I organizing my life in such a way that I have regular contact with unbelievers—so that I can share with them my faith in Jesus?

11. Discuss each of these three convictions separately, then put their total effect together. Don't neglect the explanation Jesus Himself offered in verses 8-11.

21 / I HAVE OVERCOME THE WORLD

John 16:16–33

2. Study verses 17–18.

3. a. Use this question to help your group carefully examine verses 19–24. Your group should find about nine references to grief or joy.

b. See verses 20, 22, 24.

4. Use this question to help Christ's metaphors of birth come alive. Be sensitive to those who might find this subject painful: those who suffer infertility, or who have experienced death or handicaps related to birth.

8. If your group has trouble with this question, refer to the note on John 14:14, page 89.

9. a. See verses 25–27, 32, 33.
b. See verses 28, 32, 33.

22 / JESUS PRAYS—FOR ME

John 17

2. If your group needs a follow-up question, ask, "Based on the way Jesus used the words here, how would you define 'eternal life'?"

3. If your group has trouble giving a complete answer to this question, ask, "What did Jesus have to look forward to?"

4. Be sure to read the instructions for this pencil exercise before you read the passage aloud. Or, read it aloud once at a normal speed, then again at a pace that allows this pencil drawing.

10. Possible feelings of response include: love, awe, humility, thanks, fear, responsibility, appreciation.

11. Clue phrases to propose include "so that" (verse 21), "to let" (verse 23), "in order that" (verse 26).

13. Areas of encouragement might include a sense of belonging (verses 21–23), the promise of heaven (verse 24), and God's love (verse 26).

23 / BETRAYED AND DENIED—BY FRIENDS

John 18:1–27

1. Encourage reports of both positive and negative reactions to crisis.

3. Use this question as a follow-up to the summaries of your character studies of Judas and Peter.

5. Find evidence that Jesus was active in verses 1, 4, 5, 7, 8, and 11.

9. Verses 19-23 refer to what was happening to Jesus inside the building. You will see a clearer picture of what was happening to Peter if you read verses 15–18 immediately followed by verses 25–27.

11. The "other disciple" appears in verse 15.

12. Draw on the information you learned about the faith and character of each of these men when you worked on question 2.

24 / WHAT IS TRUTH?

John 18:28–19:42

3. See John 18:28–29, 33, 38; 19:1, 4, 8–9, 12–13, along with the general purpose for each trip.

4. See John 18:29–31, 39–40; 19:1–3, 4–7, 12–16, and 19–22.

7. Your group can find possible reasons for fear in John 18:36, 40; 19:7, 12. Pilate was caught between his angry Jewish constituency (who maneuvered him into releasing the leader of a rebellion), his own higher political authorities who might accuse him of being soft on treason, and a person on trial who claimed to be the Son of the living God. And it was still early morning. No wonder Pilate was afraid.

8. See John 18:38, 39, and 19:5, 12, and 15.

10. This recurrent theme appears in 18:33, 36, 37, 39, and 19:3, 12, 14, and 19.

25 / THAT YOU MAY BELIEVE

John 20

2. Your group should speak of Mary, Simon Peter, the "other disciple"—probably John, two angels, Jesus, the group of disciples, and Thomas.

3. a. Your group should find evidences for death and resurrection in the following verses: 19:34, 38–40; 20:1, 7–9, 14–16, 18, 19–20, 26–28. It may help to keep the discussion on track if you ask group members to begin answers with, "I see the evidence of . . ."

4. Don't skimp on time as you discuss this key doctrine of the Christian faith.

5. Use these three questions to study the changes in Mary. Someone is sure to wonder, "With all the Marys in Jesus' life, which Mary is this?" She is Mary of Magdala, also mentioned in Mark 16:9 and Luke 8:2–3 (where Luke notes that she had been freed of seven demons).

9. Your group should notice Christ's invitation to Thomas—as well as Thomas's response. "My Lord and my God," had intense meaning to a Jew who believed on one God alone.

26 / DO YOU LOVE ME MORE THAN THESE?

John 21

2. If you compare John 1:35–50 with the men listed here, you see that those named (except for Thomas) lived in Galilee. Some three years earlier, Jesus had called them to be His disciples. Now they went back home—and brought

Thomas with them. Why? Several possible motives come to mind. Let your group discuss these.

4. For an outline of Peter's actions, see verses 7–9.

5. Your group should think of several related past experiences. In John 6:1–15, Jesus fed five thousand people from a boy's lunch of bread and fish. (Where did Jesus get the bread and fish for the intimate breakfast recorded here?)

In John 6:16–24, Jesus alarmed his disciples by walking three and one-half miles out to them on stormy Lake Galilee. Now it was Peter who waded a hundred yards to Jesus—through the same lake.

Of course, the meal here is a reminder of their last supper together, recorded in John 13—as well as the other gospels.

For a similar "fish story" of their past, see Luke 5:1–11.

Besides these, this simple breakfast on the shore probably re-created a score of similar meals throughout their three years of travel together.

7. Your group may have several ideas. Among them, Peter's declaration in John 13:36–38 that he would lay down his life for Jesus—and the subsequent threefold denial.

11. Jesus had completed His ministry on earth. Except for these brief appearances during the forty days after the resurrection, Peter would not see Jesus again. What then did Jesus mean when He told Peter, "Follow Me"?

Your group may have several ideas. Was Jesus echoing His invitation of John 1 inviting Peter to resume his previous position as a full-fledged disciple?

Was Jesus asking Peter to feed His "sheep" in the same way that He had?

Or was Jesus inviting Peter to follow Him in death—giving his life for the Christian faith? Peter did.

14. Your group should discuss the details of verses 24 and 25. You might also point out verses 22 and 23 where John corrects a false rumor—even one complimentary to himself.

BIBLIOGRAPHY

Aharoni, Yohanan and Michael Avi-Yonah. *The Macmillan Bible Atlas.* New York: The Macmillan Company, 1968.

Archer, Gleason L. *Encyclopedia of Bible Difficulties.* Grand Rapids: Zondervan Publishing House, 1982.

Douglas, J. D. *New Bible Dictionary.* Grand Rapids: Wm. B. Eerdmans Publishing Co., 1962.

Guthrie, C., J. A. Motyer, A. M. Stibbs, D. J. Wiseman. *New Bible Commentary.* Grand Rapids: Wm. B. Eerdmans Publishing Co., 1970.

Morris, Leon. *Commentary on the Gospel of John.* Grand Rapids: Zondervan Publishing House, 1945.

Pink, Arthur W. *Exposition of the Gospel of John.* Grand Rapids: Zondervan Publishing House, 1945.

Roberts, David. *Yesterday in the Holy Land.* Grand Rapids: Zondervan Publishing House, 1982.

Tasker, R. V. G. *The Gospel According to St. John.* Grand Rapids: Wm. B. Eerdmans Publishing Co., 1961.

Tenney, Merrill C. *John: The Gospel of Belief.* Grand Rapids: William B. Eerdmans Publishing Co., 1948.

_____."Lectures on the Gospel of John for the Louis S. Bauman Memorial Lectures at Grace Theological Seminary," February 12–15, 1974.

_____. *The New Testament: An Historical and Analytical Survey.* Grand Rapids: Wm. B. Eerdmans Publishing Co., 1953.

_____. *The Zondervan Pictorial Encyclopedia of the Bible.* Grand Rapids: Zondervan Publishing House, 1975.